Selections from
The Little Flowers
of Saint Francis
of Assisi

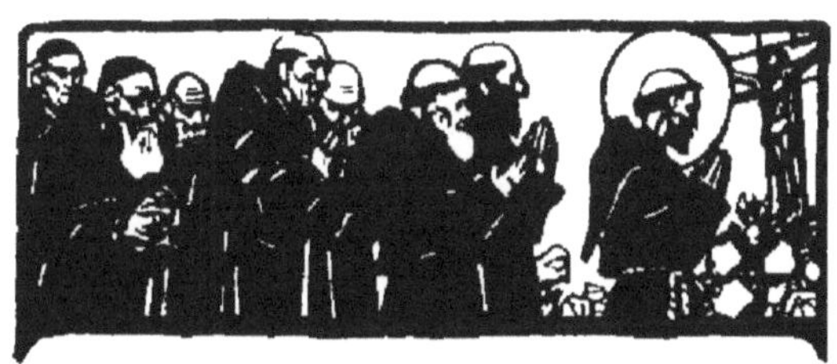

In the first English translation,
revised and emended by
Dom Roger Hudleston,
with illustrations by
Maximilian Liebenwein

A Note on This Book

YEARS AGO in Austria, I found a small rare book, called on its cover *Franz von Assisi,* and on its title page *Legenden vom Heiligen Franz.* The pocket-sized book, only 106 pages, contains selections from *The Little Flowers of Saint Francis,* translated by Karl Toth and illustrated by Maximilian Liebenwein. It appeared as part of the *Kleine Amalthea-Bücherei*—to be more precise, the third volume of the first series (*I. Reihe, III. Band*)—from the Amalthea Verlag, Zürich-Wien-Leipzig, in 1921. In small print the book tells us that there were 250 exemplars made with Japanese paper, numbered and signed by the artist, bound in leather. Since its cover and paper are made of humbler materials, my specimen was obviously not one of these (which must be priceless by now, however many happen to survive), but I was still filled with amazement when I paged through my copy. The illustrations are remarkable for their vigor, clarity, and drama, with the strong graphic design of their time period. Of particular note are the eight full-color plates, which were printed with gold, blue, and red, and then hand-colored with pencils.

That was more than 15 years ago, perhaps closer to 20, and every once in a while when I noticed the book on my shelf, I would take it down and wonder anew at its artistry. I began to feel it was a crime not to make these illustrations available to a wider public. After deciding that a facsimile would be of little use to most English speakers, I set to work compiling and gently editing stories from an elegant English translation of *The Little Flowers* in the public domain. Naturally, I began with the stories found in the original German volume, but as I went along, the charm of other stories worked on me irresistibly, and so I added them, too—hence the larger size of this volume. It is not the complete *Little Flowers,* but it delivers a respectable portion of classic stories about St. Francis and his early companions. The size of the print and the fine illustrations make it an ideal book for older children or for reading aloud in the family.

iii

In the German book, the narration of the imprinting of the stigmata of Jesus Christ upon St. Francis—an event whose repercussions we are still feeling almost 800 years later—comes near the end, but not quite at the end. In this edition I have placed the account of the stigmata, the death of Francis, and the subsequent approbation of this miracle at the very end, as this seems the most fitting way to conclude a book of stories about the man who seemed to his contemporaries to be an *alter Christus*, an embodiment of the life and death of Christ, in an altogether unprecedented way.

These stories bring us face-to-face and heart-to-heart with the *real* St. Francis and with his genuine followers: radically Catholic; ascetics, holy fools, and mystics of the Mass; enthralling in their colorfulness, yet a challenge to all of our modern assumptions and an antidote to our contemporary poisons. There is much in these pages that Catholics have forgotten and need to recover. May God grant us the grace to do so for His glory and our salvation.

I would like to thank my son, Julian, for his excellent work scanning in the illustrations, preparing the English text for editing, and doing a preliminary layout. This is the first of what we hope will be a number of books from the "Os Justi" imprint.

Peter A. Kwasniewski
Lander, Wyoming
September 27, 2016
✠ Saints Cosmas and Damian

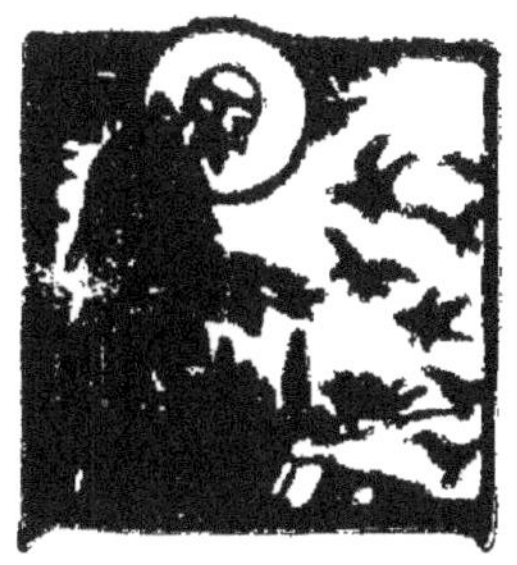

Selections from
The Little Flowers
of Saint Francis
of Assisi

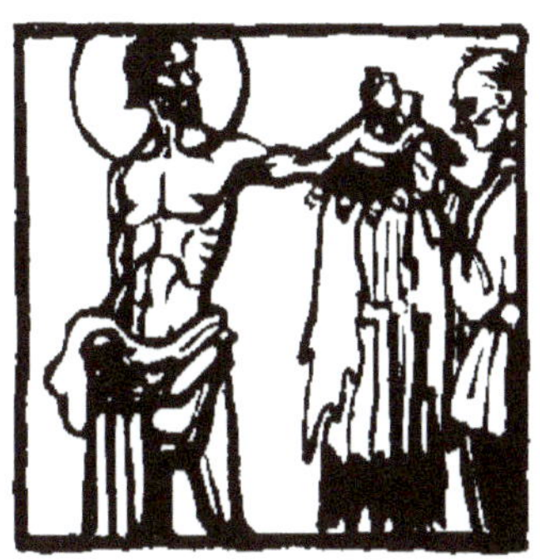

Here begin the Little Flowers of Saint Francis of Assisi

IN THE NAME OF JESUS CHRIST OUR CRUCIFIED SAVIOR, AND OF MARY HIS VIRGIN MOTHER. IN THIS BOOK ARE CONTAINED CERTAIN LITTLE FLOWERS—TO WIT, MIRACLES AND PIOUS EXAMPLES OF THE GLORIOUS SERVANT OF CHRIST SAINT FRANCIS, AND OF SOME OF HIS HOLY COMPANIONS; TO THE GLORY AND PRAISE OF JESUS CHRIST, AMEN.

FIRST LET US consider how the life of the glorious St. Francis was conformed in every act with that of our Blessed Lord. For as Christ, before He began to preach, made choice of twelve Apostles, teaching them to despise all the things of this world, to follow him in poverty and in the practice of all other virtues, so St. Francis, on the first founding of his Order, chose twelve companions, all lovers of poverty.

And even as one of the twelve Apostles, being reproved by Christ, hanged himself by the neck, so among the twelve companions of St. Francis was one, called Brother John della Capella, who apostatized, and finally hanged himself by the neck. This should be for the elect a great example and cause of humility and fear, when they consider how no one is certain of persevering in the grace of God to the end.

As the holy Apostles, being filled with the Spirit of God, shone forth mightily before the world in holiness and humility, so too did the companions of St. Francis; for from the time of the Apostles till this present day the world had never seen men so wonderful and so holy.

One of them, Brother Giles, like St. Paul, was raised to the third heaven; another, Brother Philip the Tall, like the prophet Isaiah, was touched upon the lips with a burning coal by an angel. Brother Silvester conversed with God, like one friend with another, as did Moses of old. Another, the most humble Brother Bernard, through the penetration of his intellect, reached the light of divine science, like the eagle—the emblem of St. John the Evangelist—and explained all the deepest mysteries of Holy Scripture. One there was who was sanctified and canonized in heaven, whilst still living on earth; this was Brother Ruffino, a nobleman of Assisi. And thus all bore singular marks of sanctity, as we shall see hereafter.

OF BROTHER BERNARD OF QUINTAVALLE, THE FIRST COMPANION OF SAINT FRANCIS

HE FIRST companion of St. Francis was Brother Bernard of Assisi, who was converted in the following way. St. Francis had not yet taken the religious habit, though he had renounced the world, and had so given himself to penance and mortification that many looked upon him as one out of his mind. He was scoffed at as a madman, was rejected and despised by his relations and by strangers, who threw stones and mud at him when he passed; yet he went on his way, accepting these insults as patiently as if he had been deaf and dumb.

Then Bernard of Assisi, one of the richest and most learned nobles of the city, began to consider deeply the conduct of St. Francis; how utterly he despised the world, how patiently he suffered injuries, and how his faith remained firm, though he had been for two years an object of contempt and rejected by all. He began to think and say within himself, "It is evident that this brother must have received great graces from God"; and so resolved to invite him to sup and to sleep in his house.

St. Francis having accepted the invitation, Bernard, who was resolved to contemplate the sanctity of his guest, ordered a bed to be prepared for him in his own room, where a lamp burned all night.

Now St. Francis, in order to conceal his sanctity, so soon as he entered the room, threw himself upon the bed, pretending to fall asleep. Bernard likewise soon after went to bed, and began to snore as if sleeping soundly. On this, St. Francis, thinking that Bernard was really fast asleep, got up and began to pray. Raising his hands and eyes to heaven, he exclaimed with great devotion and fervor, "My God! My God!" at the same time weeping bitterly; and thus he remained on his knees all night, repeating with great love and fervor the words, "My God! My God!" and none others. And this he did because, being enlightened by the Holy Spirit, he contemplated and admired the divine majesty of God, who deigned to take pity on the perishing world, and to save not only the soul of Francis, His poor little one, but those of many others also by means of him. For, being enlightened by the Holy Ghost, he foresaw the great things which God would deign to accomplish through him and through his Order; and considering his insufficiency and unworthiness, he prayed and called upon the Lord, through His power and wisdom, to supply, help and accomplish that which of himself he could not do.

Then Bernard, seeing by the light of the lamp the devout actions of St. Francis and the expression of his countenance, and devoutly considering the words he uttered, was touched by the Holy Spirit, and resolved to change his life.

Next morning, therefore, he called St. Francis, and thus addressed him: "Brother Francis, I am disposed in heart wholly to leave the world, and to obey thee in all things as thou shalt command me." At these words, St. Francis rejoiced in spirit and said, "Bernard, a resolution such as thou speakest of is so difficult and so great an act, that we must take counsel of the Lord Jesus Christ, and pray to Him that He may be pleased to show us what is His will, and may teach us to follow it. Let us then go together to the Bishop's palace, where we shall find a good priest who will say Mass for us. We will then remain in prayer till the third hour, imploring the Lord to point out to us the way He wishes us to select, and to this intent we will open the Missal three times." And when Bernard answered that he was well pleased with this proposal, they set out together, heard Mass, and after they had remained in prayer till the time fixed, the priest, at the request of St. Francis, took up the Missal, then, having made the sign of the holy cross, he opened it three times, in the name of our Lord Jesus Christ.

The first place which he lit upon was at the answer of Christ to the young man who asked of Him the way to perfection: *If thou wilt be perfect, go, sell all that thou hast and give to the poor, and come, follow me.*

The second time, he opened at the words which the Savior addressed to the Apostles when He sent them forth to preach the Word of Truth: *Take nothing with you for your journey: neither staff, nor scrip, nor bread, nor money;* wishing to teach them thereby to commit the care of their lives to Him, and give all their thoughts to the preaching of the Holy Gospel.

When the Missal was opened a third time they came upon these words: *If any one will come after me, let him deny himself, and take up his cross, and follow me.*

Then St. Francis, turning to Bernard, said: "This is the advice that the Lord has given us; go and do as thou hast heard; and blessed be the Lord Jesus Christ who has pointed out to thee the way of His angelic life."

Upon this, Bernard went and sold all that he had. Now he was very rich, and with great joy he distributed his wealth to widows, to orphans, to prisoners, to monasteries, to hospitals, and to pilgrims, in all of which St. Francis assisted him with prudence and fidelity.

Now it happened that a man of the name of Silvester, seeing how St. Francis gave so much money to the poor, being urged on by avarice, went to him and said: "Thou didst not pay me enough for the stones I sold thee to repair the church; now that thou hast money, pay me what thou owest." St. Francis, much surprised at such a demand, but, according to the precepts of the Scriptures, not wishing to dispute with him, gave it to Silvester, saying that, if he wanted more, he would give it to him.

Silvester, being satisfied, returned home; but in the evening of the same day he reflected on his avarice, and on the holiness and the fervor of St. Francis. That night also he saw St. Francis in a vision, and it seemed to him as if a golden cross came out of his mouth, which reached up to heaven and extended to the extreme east and west.

After this vision he gave all he possessed to the poor, for the love of God, and made himself a Brother Minor. He became so holy, and was favored with such special graces, that he spake with the Lord as a friend speaks with a friend, of which St. Francis was often a witness, as we shall see further on.

Bernard likewise received from God many graces—he was ravished in contemplation, and St. Francis said he was worthy of all reverence, and that he had founded the Order, because he was the first who had abandoned the world, giving all he possessed to the poor of Christ, keeping back nothing for himself; and practicing evangelical poverty, placing himself naked in the arms of the Crucified, whom may we all bless eternally. Amen.

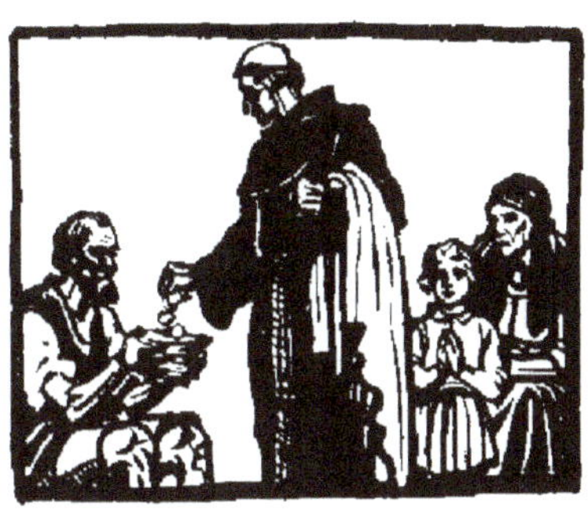

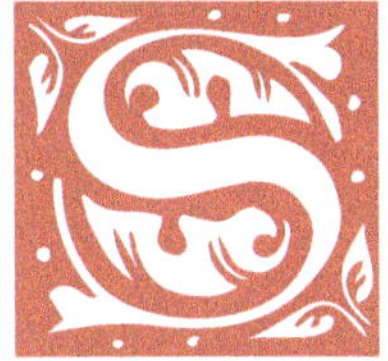

SAINT FRANCIS, when residing at Assisi, often visited St. Clare, to give her holy counsel. And she, having a great desire to eat once with him, often begged him to grant her this request; but the saint would never allow her this consolation.

His companions, therefore, being aware of the refusal of St. Francis, and knowing how great was the wish of Sister Clare to eat with him, went to seek him, and thus addressed him: "Father, it seems to us that this severity on thy part in not granting so small a thing to Sister Clare, a virgin so holy and so dear to God, who merely asks for once to eat with thee, is not according to holy charity, especially if we consider how it was at thy preaching that she abandoned the riches and pomps of this world. Of a truth, if she were to ask of thee even a greater grace than this, thou shouldst grant it to thy spiritual daughter."

St. Francis answered: "It seems to you, then, that I ought to grant her this request?"

His companions made answer: "Yea, father, it is fitting that thou grant her this favor and this consolation."

St. Francis answered: "As you think, let it be so, then; but, in order that she may be the more consoled, I will that the meal take place in front of St. Mary of the Angels, because, having been for so long time shut up in San Damiano, it will do her good to see the church of St. Mary, wherein she took the veil, and was made a spouse of Christ. There, then, we will eat together in the name of God."

When the appointed day arrived, St. Clare left her convent with great joy, taking with her one of her sisters, and followed by the companions of St. Francis. She arrived at St. Mary of the Angels, and having devoutly saluted the Virgin Mary, before whose altar her hair had been cut off and she had received the veil, they conducted her to the convent and showed her all over it.

In the meantime St. Francis prepared the meal on the bare ground, as was his custom. The hour of dinner being arrived, St. Francis and St. Clare, with one of the brethren of St. Francis and the sister who had accompanied the saint, sat down together, all the other companions of St. Francis seated humbly round them.

When the first dish was served, St. Francis began to speak of God so sweetly, so sublimely, and in a manner so wonderful, that the grace of God visited them abundantly, and all were rapt in Christ.

Whilst they were thus rapt, with eyes and hearts raised to heaven, the people of Assisi and of Bettona, and all the country round about, saw St. Mary of the Angels as it were on fire, with the convent and the woods adjoining. It seemed to them as if the church, the convent, and the woods were all enveloped in flames; and the inhabitants of Assisi hastened with great speed to put out the fire.

On arriving at the convent, they found no fire; and entering within the gates they saw St. Francis, St. Clare, with all their companions, sitting round their humble meal, absorbed in contemplation. Then they knew, of a certainty, that what they had seen was a celestial fire, not a material one, which God miraculously had sent to bear witness to the divine flame of love which consumed the souls of those holy brethren and nuns; and they returned home with great consolation in their hearts, and much holy edification.

After a long lapse of time, St. Francis, St. Clare, and their companions came back to themselves; and, being fully restored by the spiritual food, cared not to eat that which had been prepared for them; so that, the holy meal being finished, St. Clare, well accompanied, returned to San Damiano, where the sisters received her with great joy, as they had feared that St. Francis might have sent her to rule some other convent, as he had already sent St. Agnes, the sister of the saint, to be Abbess of the Convent of Monticelli at Florence. For St. Francis had often said to St. Clare, "Be ready, in case I send thee to some other convent"; and she, like a daughter of holy obedience, had answered, "Father, I am always ready to go whithersoever thou shalt send me." For which reason the sisters greatly rejoiced when she returned to them, and St. Clare was from that time much consoled.

HOW SAINT FRANCIS FOUNDED THE THIRD ORDER, PREACHED TO THE BIRDS, AND REDUCED TO SILENCE THE SWALLOWS

HE HUMBLE servant of Christ, St. Francis, a short time after his conversion, having already assembled and received many brothers into the Order, was much troubled and perplexed in mind as to what he ought to do; whether to give himself entirely to prayer, or now and then to preach the word. Through his great humility, he had no opinion of himself or of the virtue of his prayers; and, wishing to know the will of God, he sought to learn it through the prayers of others.

Wherefore he called to him Brother Masseo, and thus addressed him: "Go to Sister Clare, and bid her from me to set herself with some of the holiest of her sisters to pray the Lord that He may show me clearly whether He wills that I should preach or only keep to prayer. Then go to Brother Silvester, and ask of him the same favor."

Now Brother Silvester had been in the world, and was the same who had seen in vision a golden cross come out of St. Francis's mouth, whose height reached up to heaven and its breadth to the farthest extremities of the world. Brother Silvester was so holy, that whatever he asked of God was granted to his prayer, and very often he held converse with the Lord; so that St. Francis revered him greatly.

Then Brother Masseo did as St. Francis had commanded him, carrying the message first to St. Clare, and then to Brother Silvester, who set about praying immediately; and, having received the answer from the Lord, returned to Brother Masseo, and said to him: "The Lord says, go and tell Brother Francis that He has called him to this state not to save merely his own soul but that he may produce fruits in those of others, and that through him many souls be saved."

Having received this answer, Brother Masseo returned to Sister Clare, to ask what she had learnt from God; and she told him that she and all her companions had received from God the same answer as the Lord had given to Brother Silvester.

Then Brother Masseo hastened to St. Francis to bring him these answers; and St. Francis received him with great charity, washing his feet, and serving him at dinner. When the repast was over, he called Brother Masseo into the forest, and, kneeling down before him, put back his hood; and crossing his arms on his breast, he said to him: "What answer dost thou bring me? What does my Lord Jesus Christ order me to do?"

Brother Masseo answered: "The Lord Jesus Christ has revealed both to Brother Silvester and to Sister Clare that it is His will thou shouldst go about the world to preach; for thou hast not been called for thyself alone, but the salvation of others."

Then St. Francis, having received the answer, and knowing it to be the will of the Lord Jesus Christ, arose with fervor, saying, "Let us go in the name of God"; and taking with him Brother Masseo and Brother Agnolo, both holy men, he let himself be guided by the Spirit of God, without considering the road he took. They soon arrived at a town called Savurniano, where St. Francis began to preach, first ordering the swallows, who were calling, to keep silence until he had finished; and the swallows obeyed his voice.

He preached with such fervor that the inhabitants of the town wished to follow him out of devotion; but St. Francis would not allow them, saying: "Be not in such haste, and leave not your homes. I will tell you what you must do to save your souls." Thereupon he founded the Third Order for the salvation of all; and leaving them much consoled and well disposed to do penance, he departed thence, and reached a spot between Cannaio and Bevagno.

And as he went on his way, with great fervor, St. Francis lifted up his eyes, and saw on some trees by the wayside a great multitude of birds; and being much surprised, he said to his companions, "Wait for me here by the way, whilst I go and preach to my little sisters the birds"; and entering into the field, he began to preach to the birds which were on the ground, and suddenly all those also on the trees came round him, and all listened while St. Francis preached to them, and did not fly away until he had given them his blessing. And Brother Masseo related afterwards to Brother James of Massa how St. Francis went among them and even touched them with his garments, and how none of them moved.

Now the substance of the sermon was this: "My little sisters the birds, ye owe much to God, your Creator, and ye ought to sing His praise at all times and in all places, because He has given you liberty to fly about into all places; and though ye neither spin nor sew, He has given you a twofold and a threefold clothing for yourselves and for your offspring. Two of all your species He sent into the Ark with Noe that you might not be lost to the world; besides which, He feeds you, though ye neither sow nor reap. He has given you fountains and rivers to quench your thirst, mountains and valleys in which to take refuge, and trees in which to build your nests; so that your Creator loves you much, having thus favored you with such bounties. Beware, my little sisters, of the sin of ingratitude, and study always to give praise to God."

As he said these words, all the birds began to open their beaks, to stretch their necks, to spread their wings and reverently to bow their heads to the ground, endeavoring by their motions and by their songs to manifest their joy to St. Francis. And the saint rejoiced with them. He wondered to see such a multitude of birds, and was charmed with their beautiful variety, with their attention and familiarity, for all which he devoutly gave thanks to the Creator.

Having finished his sermon, St. Francis made the sign of the cross, and gave them leave to fly away. Then all those birds rose up into the air, singing most sweetly; and, following the sign of the cross, which St. Francis had made, they divided themselves into four companies. One company flew towards the east, another towards the west, one towards the south,

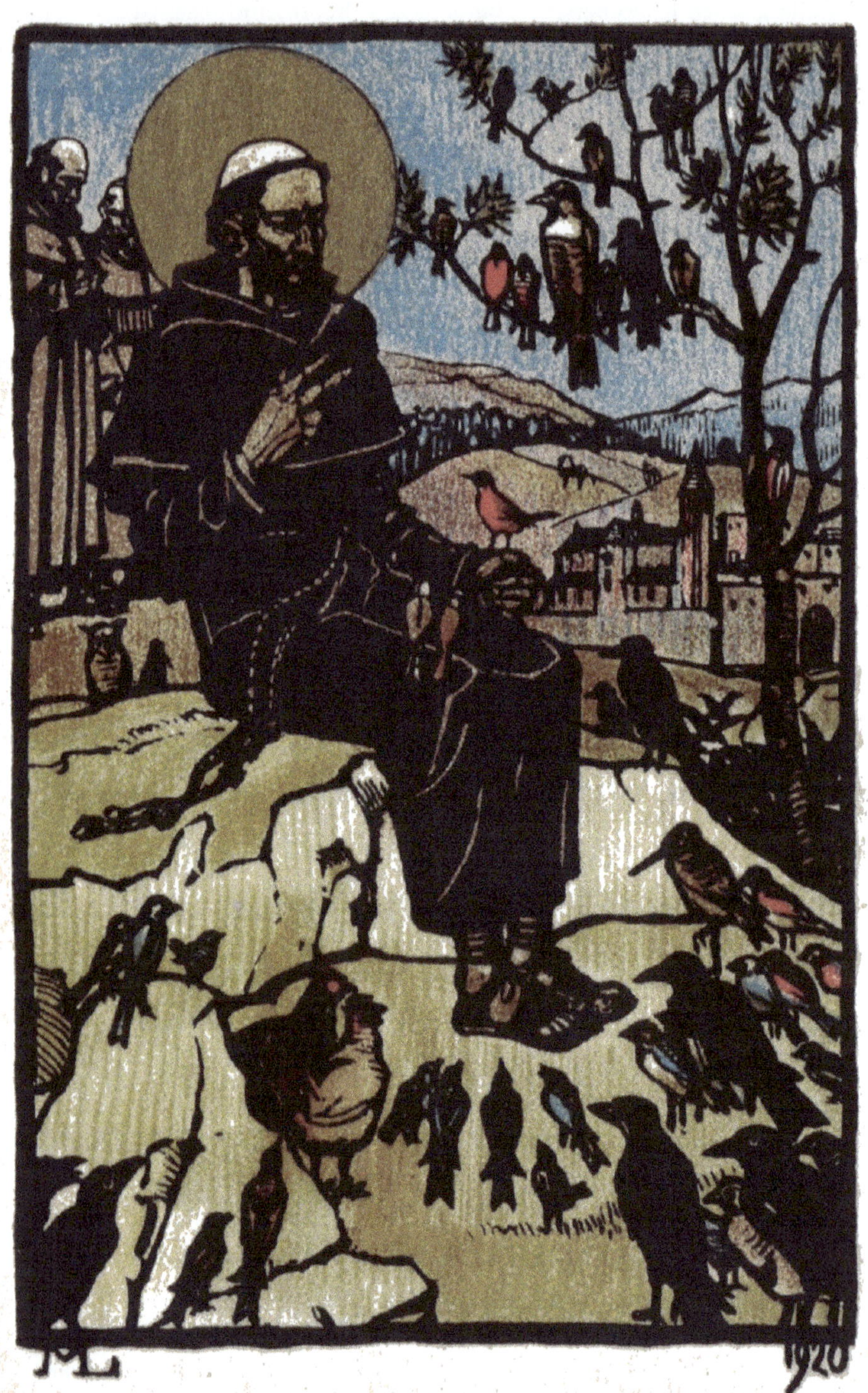

and one towards the north, each company as it went singing most wonderfully, signifying thereby that as St. Francis, the bearer of the Cross of Christ, had preached to them and made upon them the sign of the cross, after which they had divided among themselves the four parts of the world, so the preaching of the Cross of Christ, renewed by St. Francis, would be carried by him and by his brethren over all the world, and that the humble friars, like little birds, should possess nothing in this world, but should cast all the care of their lives on the providence of God.

HOW A LITTLE CHILD WHO HAD ENTERED THE ORDER SAW SAINT FRANCIS IN PRAYER ONE NIGHT, AND SAW ALSO THE SAVIOR, THE VIRGIN MARY, AND MANY OTHER SAINTS TALK WITH HIM

CERTAIN pure and innocent child was received into the Order during the lifetime of St. Francis, and the convent in which he lived was so small that the monks were obliged to sleep on mats. It chanced that St. Francis came one day to that convent, and in the evening, after Compline, he went to rest, so as to rise up early to pray, as was his custom, when all the other friars were still asleep. The said little child had made up his mind carefully to watch St. Francis, to learn something of his sanctity, and find out more especially what he did in the night when he got up; and in order that he might not be overtaken by sleep, he laid him down by St. Francis, tying the end of the cord he wore round his waist to the one which the saint wore, so that he was sure of being awakened when the latter got up in the night; and this he did so gently, that St. Francis was not aware of his contrivance.

When all the other friars were fast asleep, St. Francis rose from sleep, and finding the child's cord tied to his own, he carefully untied it so as not to awake him and went alone into the wood which was near the convent. Entering into a little cell which was there, he began to pray. Shortly after, the child awoke, and finding St. Francis gone, and the cord untied, he rose up quickly and went to seek him.

Perceiving the door open which led to the wood, he thought St. Francis had gone that way; and entering into the wood, and hurrying on to

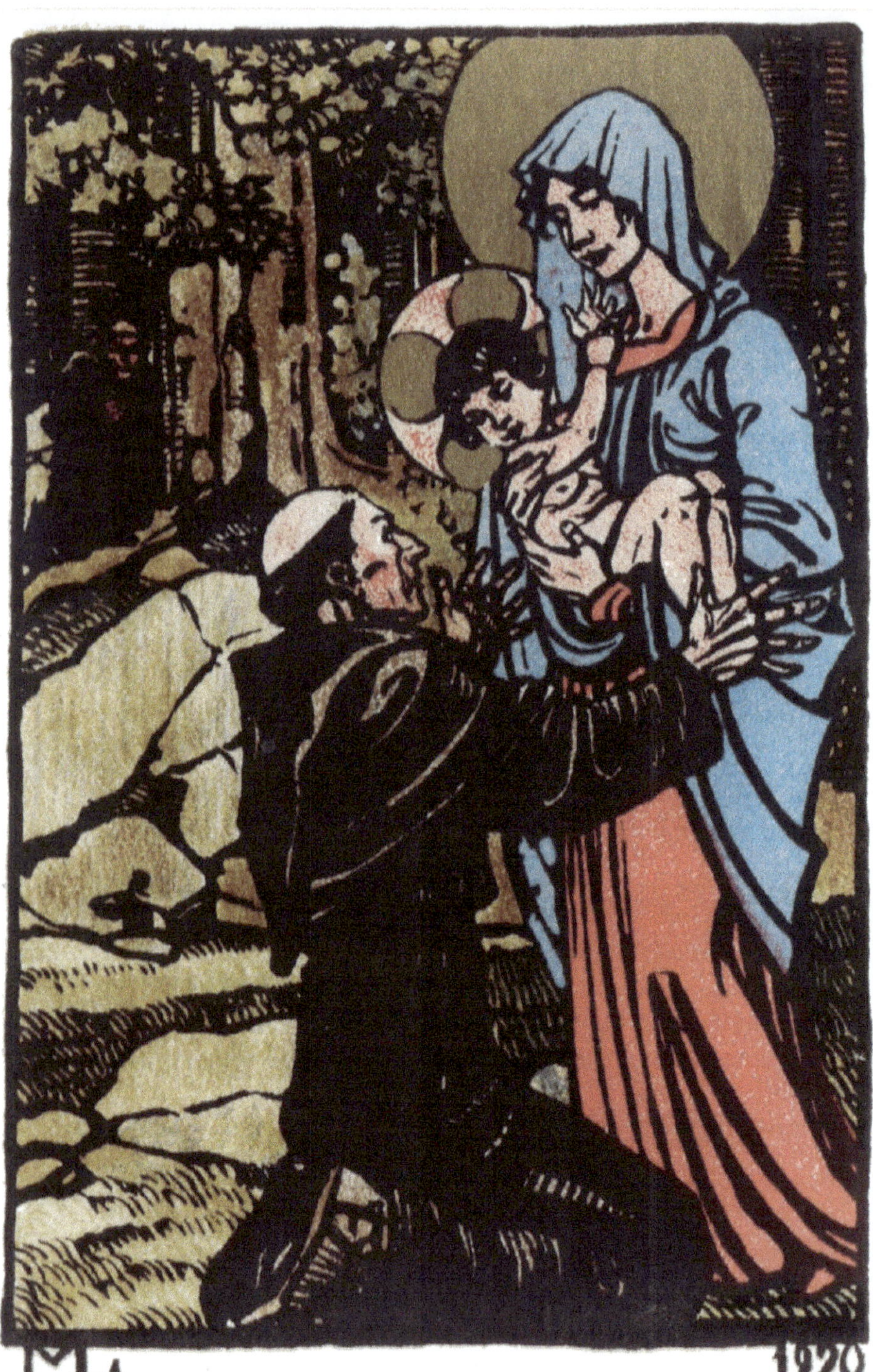

ML
1920

to the little cell, he heard the sound of many voices. Approaching near to hear and see whence they came, he saw a great and wonderful light all round the saint, and in the light was Jesus Christ, with the Virgin Mary, St. John the Baptist, St. John the Evangelist, and a great multitude of angels, all talking with St. Francis. On seeing this the child fell to the ground as if he had been dead.

The miracle of this holy vision being ended, St. Francis rose to return to the convent, and stumbling in the way against the child, who appeared to be dead, with great compassion he took him up in his arms and carried him in his bosom, as the good shepherd is wont to carry his lambs.

Having learned from him how he had seen the vision, he forbade him to tell any man thereof so long as he, St. Francis, lived. The little child grew up in the grace of God, and had a great devotion to St. Francis. He became one of the most distinguished men of the Order. After the death of St. Francis, he related the vision to the brethren.

OF THE WONDERFUL CHAPTER HELD BY SAINT FRANCIS AT SAINT MARY OF THE ANGELS, AT WHICH MORE THAN FIVE THOUSAND FRIARS WERE PRESENT

HE FAITHFUL servant of Christ, St. Francis, once held a general chapter at St. Mary of the Angels, at which chapter more than five thousand friars were present. Amongst them also was St. Dominic, the head and founder of the Order of Friars Preachers, who chanced to be on his way from Bologna to Rome: for having heard of the chapter which St. Francis had called together in the plain of St. Mary of the Angels, he went there with seven friars of his Order.

A certain Cardinal also, much devoted to St. Francis, to whom the saint had foretold that he would one day be Pope, came expressly from Perugia to Assisi, and every day he went to visit St. Francis and his brethren. Sometimes he sang Mass and preached to them; and each time the said Cardinal visited the holy company, he experienced much pleasure and devotion.

Seeing the friars all seated in the plain round St. Mary of the Angels, in groups—here forty, there a hundred, and elsewhere eighty, all occupied in conversing about God, or in prayer, or in works of charity—seeing them all so silent and so grave, and wondering how such a multitude could be so orderly, he was moved to tears, and exclaimed, with great devotion, "Truly this is the field of God; this is the army, and these are the knights of the Lord." No vain or useless word was to be heard in all that multitude; each group of friars was engaged either in prayer, or saying their office, in weeping over their sins and those of their benefactors, or in reasoning on the salvation of souls.

Many tents made of mats had been pitched in that field, divided in groups, according to the different provinces from whence the friars came; so that this chapter was called the "Chapter of Mats." The friars had no other beds but the bare ground, with here and there a little straw; for pillows they had stones or pieces of wood. For which reasons they were held in much devotion; and so great was the fame of their sanctity, that many came to see and hear them from the court of the Pope which was at Perugia, and from other parts of the valley of Spoleto. Many counts and barons, many knights and other gentlemen, many Cardinals, Bishops, and Abbots, many priests and much people, came to see this great and holy and humble congregation, for the world had never yet witnessed so many holy men assembled together. And most especially they went thither to see the saintly founder and father of the Order, who had taken from the world so many gifted men, and had formed so beautiful and devout a flock to follow the steps of the true Pastor, Jesus Christ.

The chapter being assembled, St. Francis, the father of all those holy men, expounded with great fervor of spirit the Word of God, speaking to them in a loud voice that which the Holy Spirit dictated. Now the subject he took for his sermon was this: "My children, we have promised great things to God, and God has promised even greater things to us. If we observe what we have promised Him, we shall certainly receive what He has promised to us. The pleasures of this world pass quickly away, but the punishment which follows them is eternal. The sufferings of this world are trifling, but the glory of the life to come is without bounds."

And, preaching on these words most devoutly, he comforted the brethren, encouraging them to practice holy obedience, to reverence Holy Mother Church, to keep charity among themselves, to pray God for all people, to bear with patience the adversities of life, to be temperate in prosperity, to keep angelic purity and chastity, to be at peace with God, with men and with their own conscience, to love, to observe, and to practice holy poverty.

He then added: "I command you all here present, through holy obedience, to take no thought what you shall eat or what you shall drink, or of aught else that is necessary to the body, but only to meditate, to pray, and to praise God, casting on Him the thought of all the rest, for He has you all in His special care; and let each of you receive this command with a happy heart and a joyful countenance."

St. Francis having finished his sermon, all the friars began to pray. Yet St. Dominic, who was present, wondered much at this order of St. Francis, considering it as indiscreet, for he could not understand how such a great multitude could exist without taking thought for the body.

But the heavenly Pastor, our Blessed Savior, wishing to show the care He takes of His lambs, and with what singular love He loves His poor servants, put into the hearts of all the people of Perugia, of Spoleto, of Foligno, of Spello, of Assisi, and of all the neighboring country, to take meat and drink to that holy congregation; and presently men came from all these places with horses, and asses, and carts laden with bread and wine, with beans and cheese, and other good things of which the poor of Christ had need. Besides all this, they brought napkins and knives, jugs and glasses, and all that was needed for such a multitude; and those who could carry most and serve the best rejoiced greatly, and the knights, barons, and other noblemen who were present waited on the brethren with great devotion and humility.

St. Dominic, seeing this, and knowing of a certainty that it was the divine providence of God which had provided for them thus, acknowledged most humbly that he had unjustly accused St. Francis of giving indiscreet orders; and going to him, he knelt humbly before him and confessed his fault, adding: "The Lord truly hath special care of all these holy servants of poverty. I knew it not till now, and henceforth I promise to observe holy evangelical poverty; and, in the name of God, I condemn all friars of my Order who shall seek to have possessions of their own." And St. Dominic was greatly edified by the faith of the most holy Francis, by the obedience and poverty of so large and well-ordered a chapter, and he blessed the providence of God, who had given them every grace in such abundance.

In that same chapter also it was revealed to St. Francis that many brethren wore on their flesh small hearts and bands of iron, for which reason many were ill and hindered in their prayers; and St. Francis, like a discreet father, gave order, under holy obedience, that all who wore such things should take them off and place them before him, and more than five hundred little hearts and bands of iron were placed before him—some destined to be worn round the arms, and others round the waist—and all together formed a large heap, which St. Francis ordered to be left in that field.

The chapter being ended, he encouraged them all in well-doing, warning them to avoid sin in this wicked world, and sent them to their diverse provinces, with his blessing and that of God, filled with spiritual joy and consolation.

HOW THE VINE OF THE PRIEST OF RIETI, WHOSE HOUSE SAINT FRANCIS ENTERED TO PRAY, WAS TRAMPLED UNDER FOOT BY THE GREAT NUMBERS WHO CAME TO SEE HIM, AND HOW IT YET PRODUCED A GREATER QUANTITY OF WINE THAN USUAL, AS SAINT FRANCIS HAD PROMISED; AND HOW THE LORD REVEALED TO THE SAINT THAT HEAVEN WOULD BE HIS PORTION WHEN HE LEFT THIS WORLD

AINT Francis at one time being grievously tormented with a disease in his eyes, the Cardinal Ugolino, protector of his Order, who loved him dearly, wrote to him to come to Rieti, where there were excellent oculists. St. Francis, having received the Cardinal's letter, set off first to San Damiano, where was Sister Clare, the devout spouse of Christ, to give her some spiritual consolation, intending afterwards to go on to the Cardinal.

On arriving at San Damiano, the following night his eyes grew so much worse that he could not see the light, and was obliged to give up going any further. Then Sister Clare made him a little cell of reeds, in order that he might repose the better; but St. Francis, owing partly to the pain he suffered, and partly to the multitude of rats, which much annoyed him, could rest neither day nor night.

After suffering for several days this pain and tribulation, he began to think that it was sent to him by God as a punishment for his sins, and he thanked the Lord in his heart and with his lips, crying out with a loud voice: "My God, I am worthy of this, and even worse. My Lord Jesus Christ, Thou Good Shepherd, who hast shown Thy mercy to us poor sinners in the various bodily pains and sufferings it pleaseth Thee to send us; grant to me, Thy little lamb, that no pain, however great, no infirmity nor anguish, shall ever separate me from Thee."

Having made this prayer, a voice came from heaven, which said: "Francis, if all the earth were of gold, if all the seas and all the fountains and all the rivers were of balm, if all mountains, all hills, and all rocks were made of precious stones, and if thou couldst find a treasure as much more precious again as gold is more precious than earth, and balm than water, and gems than mountains and rocks, if that precious treasure were offered to thee in the place of thy infirmity, wouldst thou not rejoice and be content?"

St. Francis answered: "Lord, I am unworthy of such a treasure."

And the voice of God said again: "Rejoice with all thy heart, Francis, for such a treasure is life eternal, which I have in keeping for thee, and even now promise to thee; and this thine infirmity and affliction is a pledge of that blessed treasure."

Then was St. Francis filled with joy at so glorious a promise; and calling his companion, he said to him: "Let us go to the Cardinal."

He humbly took leave of Sister Clare, after having comforted her with holy words, and took the road to Rieti.

When he approached the town, such a multitude came out to meet him, that he would not go into the city, but went to a church which was about two miles off. But the people, hearing where he was gone, went thither to see him; so that the vine which surrounded the church was greatly injured, and all the grapes were gathered; at which the priest, to whom it belonged, was very grieved in his heart, and repented of having received St. Francis in his church.

The thought of the priest being revealed to the saint, he called him to him and said: "Dearest father, tell me, how many measures of wine does this vine produce when the year is a fertile one?" He answered: "Twelve measures." Then said St. Francis: "I pray thee, father, have patience and endure my presence here a few days longer, as I find great rest in this church; and, for the love of God and of me His poor servant, let the people gather the grapes off thy vine; for I promise thee, in the name of my Savior Jesus Christ, that it shall produce every year twenty measures of wine."

And St. Francis remained there for the benefit of the souls of all who went to see him, for many went away filled with divine love, and gave up the world.

The priest, having faith in the promise of St. Francis, left the vineyard open to all those who came to see him. And, wonder of wonders!, although the vine was entirely ruined, so that there scarcely remained, here and there, a few small bunches of grapes, when the time of vintage arrived, the priest gathered the few bunches which were left, and put them into the winepress; and according to the promise of St. Francis, these few little bunches did not fail to produce twenty measures of excellent wine.

This miracle teaches us that as, in consequence of the merits of St. Francis, the vine, though despoiled of its grapes, produced an abundance of wine, so in the same way many Christians, whose sins had made them barren of virtue, through the saint's preaching and merits, have often come to abound in the good fruit of repentance.

 YOUNG MAN, of noble birth, and of delicate habits, who had entered the Order of St. Francis, was seized after a few days, through the devil's suggestions, with a violent dislike of the habit that he wore: he hated the shape of the sleeves; he felt a horror for the hood, for the length of the dress, and the coarseness of the material; so that it seemed to him

as if he carried about him an insupportable weight; and, disliking the Order more and more, he determined to leave it and return to the world.

It was the custom of this young man, at whatever hour he passed before the altar in the convent at which the Blessed Sacrament was reserved, to kneel down with great respect and, covering his head with his hood and crossing his arms on his breast, to prostrate himself, as he had been taught to do by the master of novices.

It so happened, that the night when he had made up his mind to leave the convent, he passed before the altar, and, kneeling down as he was wont to do, he prostrated himself to the ground, and, being ravished in spirit, the Lord sent him a most wonderful vision. He saw before him a great multitude of saints ranged in procession, two by two, clothed in vestments made of precious material: their faces and their hands shone like the sun; they sang, as they walked, to the sound of celestial music. Two of them were more nobly and more richly dressed than the rest, and surrounded by such a blaze of light that none could look on them without being dazzled. At the end of the procession was one so gloriously adorned, that he seemed, like a new knight, to be more favored than the others.

Now the young man, seeing such a beautiful procession, was struck with wonder; but although he could not guess the meaning of the vision, he dared not ask, and seemed struck dumb with amazement. When the procession had almost passed away, he took courage, and addressing himself to those who were in the rear, he said: "O beloved, I pray you tell me who are those wonderful beings who form this venerable procession."

They answered: "Know, my son, that we are all Friars Minor, who are come from the glories of paradise; and those two who shine forth brighter than the rest are St. Francis and St. Anthony; and the last one you saw so especially honored is a holy friar, lately dead, who having fought with courage against temptation and having preserved to the end, we lead in triumph to the glories of paradise; and these splendid vestments which adorn us have been given to us by God, in exchange for the coarse tunic we wore with so much patience in religion; and the glorious light which shines upon us has been given in reward for the humility, the holy poverty, the obedience, and chastity that we observed to the end of our lives. Now, my son, do not find the robe of religion too rough to wear; for if, clothed in the sackcloth of St. Francis, and out of love to Christ, thou dost despise the world, mortifying thy flesh, and fighting valiantly against the devil, thou too shalt receive these splendid vestments, and shine with this glorious light."

On hearing these words the young man came to his senses, and feeling himself much strengthened, he put far from him all temptation to leave the Order, confessed his sin to the guardian and to the brethren, and from that moment dearly loved the course vestment of St. Francis and the severity of penance, and at length ended his life in the Order in a state of great sanctity.

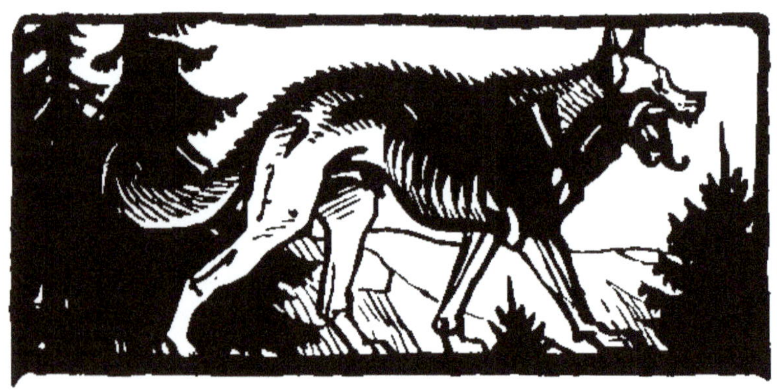

OF THE MOST HOLY MIRACLE OF SAINT FRANCIS IN TAMING THE FIERCE WOLF OF GUBBIO

AT THE TIME when St. Francis was living in the city of Gubbio, a large wolf appeared in the neighborhood, so terrible and so fierce, that he not only devoured other animals, but made a prey of men also; and since he often approached the town, all the people were in great alarm, and used to go about armed, as if going to battle. Notwithstanding these precautions, if any of the inhabitants ever met him alone, he was sure to be devoured, as all defenses was useless: and, through fear of the wolf, they dared not go beyond the city walls.

St. Francis, feeling great compassion for the people of Gubbio, resolved to go and meet the wolf, though all advised him not to do so. Making the sign of the holy cross, and putting all his confidence in God, he went forth from the city, taking his brethren with him; but these fearing to go any further, St. Francis bent his steps alone toward the spot where the wolf was known to be, while many people followed at a distance, and witnessed the miracle.

The wolf, seeing all this multitude, ran towards St. Francis with his jaws wide open. As he approached, the saint, making the sign of the cross, cried out: "Come hither, brother wolf; I command thee, in the name of Christ, neither to harm me nor anybody else." Marvelous to tell, no sooner had St. Francis made the sign of the cross, than the terrible wolf, closing his jaws, stopped running, and coming up to St. Francis, lay down at his feet as meekly as a lamb.

And the saint thus addressed him: "Brother wolf, thou hast done much evil in this land, destroying and killing the creatures of God without His permission; yea, not animals only hast thou destroyed, but thou hast even dared to devour men, made after the image of God; for which thing thou art worthy of being hanged like a robber and a murderer. All men cry out against thee, the dogs pursue thee, and all the inhabitants of this city are thy enemies; but I will make peace between them and thee, O brother wolf, if so be thou no more offend them, and they shall forgive thee all thy past offences, and neither men nor dogs shall pursue thee any more."

Having listened to these words, the wolf bowed his head, and, by the movements of his body, his tail, and his eyes, made signs that he agreed to what St. Francis said. On this St. Francis added: "As thou art willing to make this peace, I promise thee that thou shalt be fed every day by the inhabitants of this land so long as thou shalt live among them; thou shalt no longer suffer hunger, as it is hunger which has made thee do so much evil; but if I obtain all this for thee, thou must promise, on thy side, never again to attack any animal or any human being; dost thou make this promise?" Then the wolf, bowing his head, made a sign that he consented.

Said St. Francis again: "Brother wolf, wilt thou pledge thy faith that I may trust to this thy promise?," and putting out his hand he received the pledge of the wolf; for the latter lifted up his paw and placed it familiarly in the hand of St. Francis, giving him thereby the only pledge which was in his power. Then said St. Francis, addressing him again: "Brother wolf, I command thee, in the name of Christ, to follow me immediately, without hesitation or doubting, that we may go together to ratify this peace

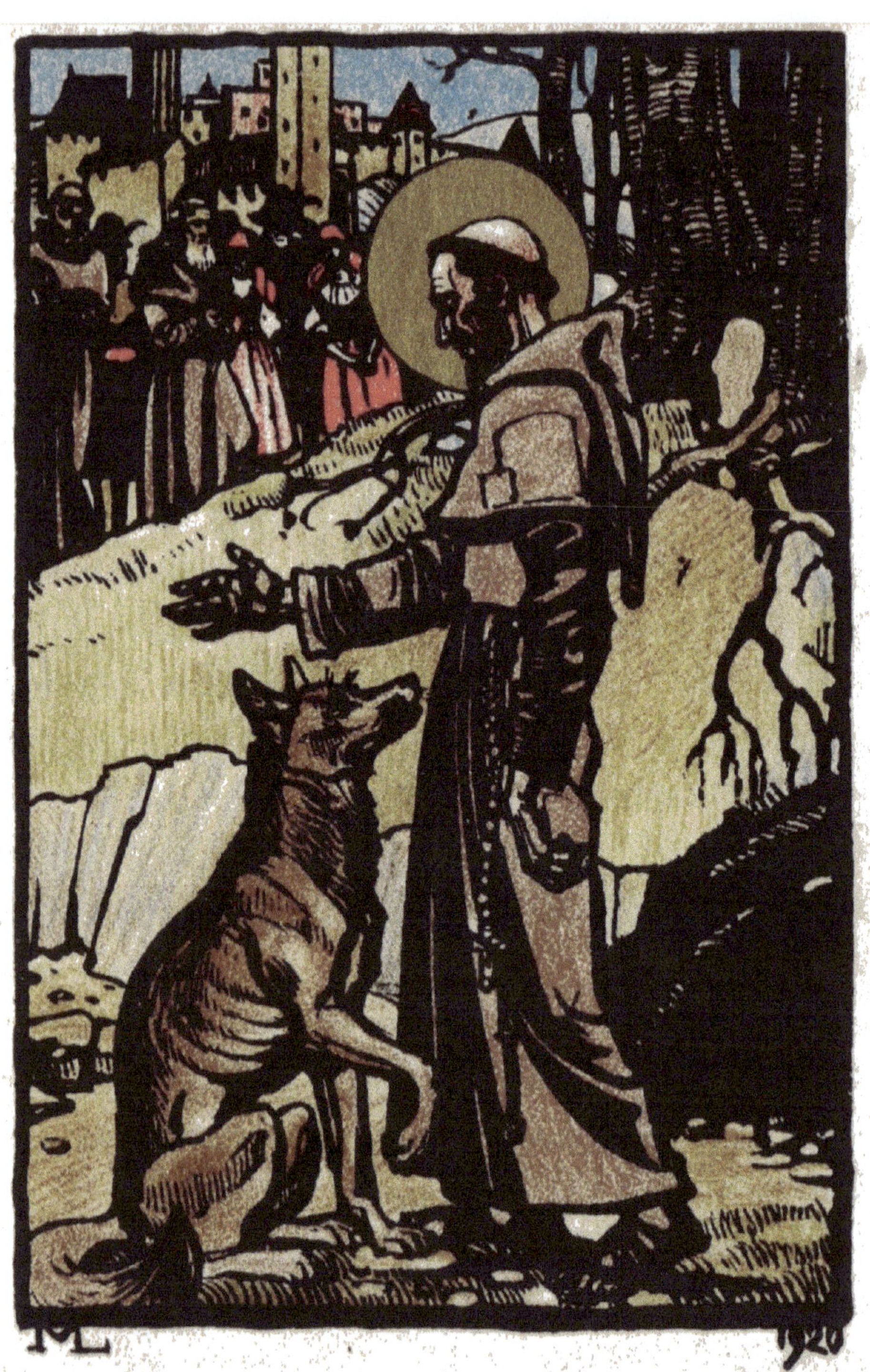

which we have concluded in the name of God"; and the wolf, obeying him, walked by his side as meekly as a lamb, to the great astonishment of all the people.

Now, the news of this most wonderful miracle spreading quickly through the town, all the inhabitants, both men and women, small and great, young and old, flocked to the market-place to see St. Francis and the wolf. All the people being assembled, the saint got up to preach, saying, amongst other things, how for our sins God permits such calamities, and how much greater and more dangerous are the flames of hell, which last for ever, than the rage of a wolf, which can kill the body only; and how much we ought to dread the jaws of hell, if the jaws of so small an animal as a wolf can make a whole city tremble through fear.

The sermon being ended, St. Francis added these words: "Listen my brethren: the wolf who is here before you has promised and pledged his faith that he consents to make peace with you all, and no more to offend you in aught, and you must promise to give him each day his necessary food; to which, if you consent, I promise in his name that he will most faithfully observe the compact."

Then all the people promised with one voice to feed the wolf to the end of his days; and St. Francis, addressing the latter, said again: "And thou, brother wolf, dost thou promise to keep the compact, and never again to offend either man or beast, or any other creature?" And the wolf knelt down, bowing his head, and, by the motions of his tail and of his ears, endeavored to show that he was willing, so far as was in his power, to hold to the compact.

Then St. Francis continued: "Brother wolf, as thou gravest me a pledge of this thy promise when we were outside the town, so now I will that thou renew it in the sight of all this people, and assure me that I have done well to promise in thy name"; and the wolf lifting up his paw placed it in the hand of St. Francis.

Now this event caused great joy in all the people, and a great devotion towards St. Francis, both because of the novelty of the miracle, and because of the peace which had been concluded with the wolf; and they lifted up their voices to heaven, praising and blessing God, who had sent them St. Francis, through whose merits they had been delivered from such a savage beast.

The wolf lived two years at Gubbio; he went familiarly from door to door without harming anyone, and all the people received him courteously, feeding him with great pleasure, and no dog barked at him as he went about. At last, after two years, he died of old age, and the people of Gubbio mourned his loss greatly; for when they saw him going about so gently amongst them all, he reminded them of the virtue and sanctity of St. Francis.

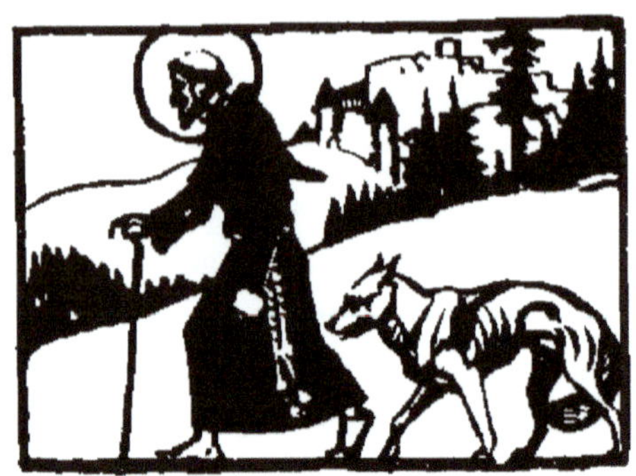

HOW SAINT FRANCIS TAMED THE WILD DOVES

CERTAIN young man having caught one day a great number of doves, as he was to sell them he met St. Francis, who always felt a great compassion for such gentle animals; and, looking at the doves with eyes of pity, he said to the young man: "O good man, I entreat thee to give me those harmless birds, emblems in Scripture of humble, pure, and faithful souls, so that they may not fall into cruel hands, which would put them to death." And the young man, inspired by God, immediately gave them to St. Francis, who, placing them in his bosom, addressed them thus sweetly: "O my little sisters the doves, so simple, so innocent, and so chaste, why did you allow yourselves to be caught? I will save you from death, and make your nests, that you may increase and multiply, according to the command of God."

Then St. Francis made nests for them all, and they began to lay their eggs and hatch them in presence of the brethren, and were as familiar and as tame with St. Francis and the friars as if they had been hens brought up amongst them, nor did they ever go away until St. Francis had given them his blessing.

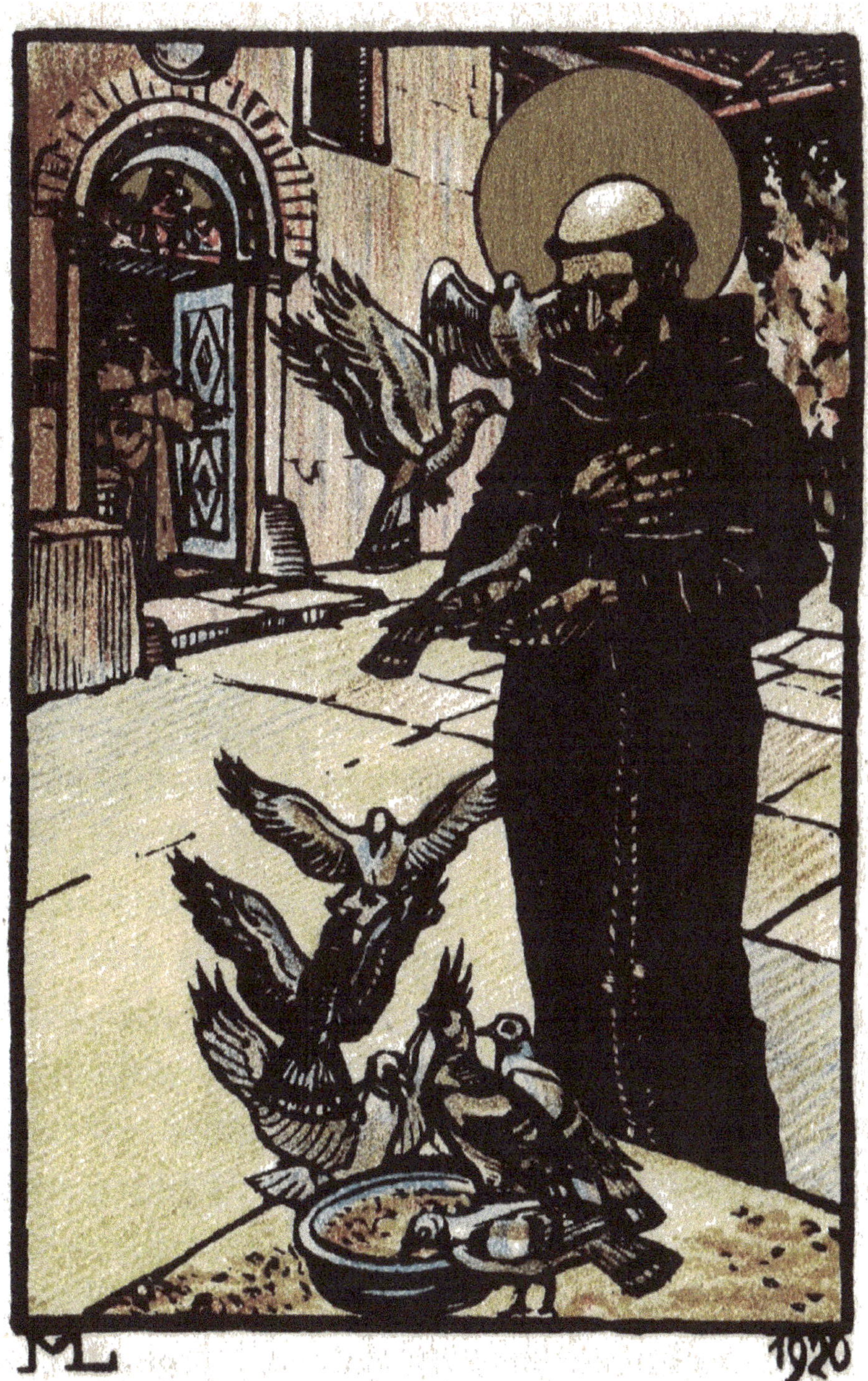

Then said St. Francis to the young man who had given them to him: "My son, thou shalt become a friar in this Order; and shalt serve most fervently the Lord Jesus Christ"; and so it came to pass, for the young man became a friar, and lived in the Order in great holiness.

HOW SAINT FRANCIS CONVERTED TO THE FAITH THE SULTAN OF BABYLON

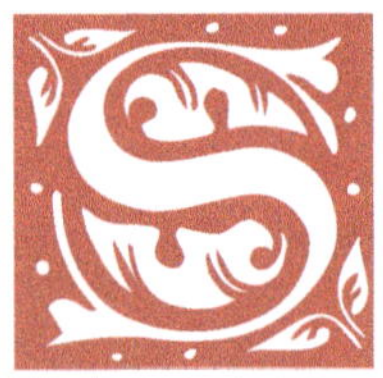

AINT FRANCIS, urged by zeal for the faith of Christ and by a wish to suffer martyrdom, took with him one day twelve of his most holy brethren, and went beyond the sea with the intention of going straight to the Sultan of Babylon.

They arrived in a province belonging to the Saracens, where all the passes were guarded by men so cruel, that no Christian who passed that way could escape being put to death. Now it pleased God that St. Francis and his companions should not meet with the same fate; but they were taken prisoners, and after being bound and ill-treated, were led before the Sultan.

Then St. Francis standing before him, inspired by the Holy Spirit, preached most divinely the faith of Christ; and to prove the truth of what he said, professed himself ready to enter into the fire. Now the Sultan began to feel a great devotion towards him, both because of the constancy of his faith, and because he despised the things of this world (for he had refused to accept any of the presents which he had offered to him), and also because of his ardent wish to suffer martyrdom. From that moment he listened to him willingly, and begged him to come back often, giving both him and his companions leave to preach wheresoever they pleased; he likewise gave them a token of his protection, which would preserve them from all molestation.

At length St. Francis, seeing he could do no more good in those parts, was warned by God to return with his brethren to the land of the faithful. Having assembled his companions, they went together to the Sultan to take leave of him. The Sultan said to him: "Brother Francis, most willingly would I be converted to the faith of Christ; but I fear to do so now, for if the people knew it, they would kill both me and thee and all

26

thy companions. As thou mayest still do much good, and I have certain affairs of great importance to conclude, I will not at present be the cause of thy death and of mine. But teach me how I can be saved, and I am ready to do as thou shalt order."

On this St. Francis made answer: "My lord, I will take leave of thee for the present; but after I have returned to my own country, when I shall be dead and gone to heaven, by the grace of God, I will send thee two of my friars, who will administer to thee the holy baptism of Christ, and thou shalt be saved, as the Lord Jesus has revealed to me; and thou in the meantime shalt free thyself from every hindrance, so that, when the grace of God arrives, thou mayest be found well disposed to faith and devotion."

The Sultan promised so to do; and did as he had promised. Then St. Francis returned with his company of venerable and saintly brethren, and after a few years ending his mortal life, he gave up his soul to God. The Sultan, having fallen ill, awaited the fulfillment of the promise of St. Francis, and placed guards in all the passes, ordering them if they met two brothers in the habit of St. Francis to conduct them immediately to him.

At the same time St. Francis appeared to two of his friars, and ordered them without delay to go to the Sultan and save his soul, according to the promise he had made him. The two set out, and having crossed the sea, were conducted to the Sultan by the guards he had sent out to meet them.

The Sultan, when he saw them arrive, rejoiced greatly, and exclaimed: "Now I know of a truth that God has sent his servants to save my soul, according to the promise which St. Francis made me through divine revelation." Having received the faith of Christ and holy baptism from the said friars, he was regenerated in the Lord Jesus Christ; and having died of his disease, his soul was saved, through the merits and prayers of St. Francis.

HE TRUE disciple of Christ, St. Francis, as long as he lived in this miserable life, endeavored with all his might to follow the example of Christ the perfect Master; whence it happened often, through the operation of grace, that he healed the soul at the same time as the body, as we read of Jesus Christ Himself; and not only did he willingly serve the lepers himself, but he willed that all the brethren of his Order, both when they were travelling about the world and when they were halting on their way, should serve the lepers for the love of Christ, who for our sake was willing to be treated as a leper.

It happened once, that in a convent near the one in which St. Francis then resided there was a hospital for leprosy and other infirmities, served by the brethren; and one of the patients was a leper so impatient, so insupportable, and so insolent, that many believed of a certainty that he was possessed of the devil (as indeed he was), for he ill-treated with blows and words all those who served him; and, what was worse, he blasphemed so dreadfully our Blessed Lord and His most holy Mother the Blessed Virgin Mary, that none was found who could or would serve him. The brethren, indeed, to gain merit, endeavored to accept with patience the injuries and violences committed against themselves, but their consciences would not allow them to submit to those addressed to Christ and to His Mother, wherefore they determined to abandon this leper, but this they would not do until they had signified their intention to St. Francis, according to the Rule.

On learning this, St. Francis, who was not far distant, himself visited this perverse leper, and said to him: "May God give thee peace, my beloved brother!"

To this the leper answered: "What peace can I look for from God, who has taken from me peace and every other blessing, and made me a putrid and disgusting object?"

St. Francis answered: "My son, be patient; for the infirmities of the body are given by God in this world for the salvation of the soul in the next; there is great merit in them when they are patiently endured."

The sick man answered: "How can I bear patiently the pain which afflicts me night and day? For not only am I greatly afflicted by my infirmity, but the friars thou hast sent to serve me make it even worse, for they do not serve me as they ought."

Then St. Francis, knowing through divine revelation that the leper was possessed by the malignant spirit, began to pray, interceding most earnestly for him. Having finished his prayer, he returned to the leper and said to him: "My son, I myself will serve thee, seeing thou art not satisfied with the others."

"Willingly," answered the leper; "but what canst thou do more than they have done?"

"Whatsoever thou wishest I will do for thee," answered St. Francis.

"I will then," said he, "that thou wash me all over; for I am so disgusting that I cannot bear myself."

Then St. Francis heated some water, putting therein many odoriferous herbs; he then undressed him, and began to wash him with his own hands, whilst another brother threw the water upon him, and, by a divine miracle, wherever St. Francis touched him with his holy hands the leprosy disappeared, and his flesh was perfectly healed also.

On this the leper, seeing his leprosy beginning to vanish, felt great sorrow and repentance for his sins, and began to weep bitterly. While his body was being purified externally of the leprosy through the cleansing of the water, so his soul internally was purified from sin by the washing of tears and repentance; and feeling himself completely healed both in his body and his soul, he humbly confessed his sins, crying out in a loud voice, with many tears: "Unhappy me! I am worthy of hell for the wickedness of my conduct to the brethren, and the impatience and blasphemy I have uttered against the Lord"; and for fifteen days he ceased not to weep bitterly for his sins, imploring the Lord to have mercy on him, and then made a general confession to a priest.

St. Francis, perceiving this evident miracle which the Lord had enabled him to work, returned thanks to God, and set out for a distant country; for out of humility he wished to avoid all glory, and in all his actions he sought only the glory of God, and not his own.

It pleased God that the leper, who had been healed both in his body and in his soul, after having done penance for fifteen days, should fall ill of another infirmity; and having received the sacraments of the Church, he died a most holy death.

His soul on its way to heaven appeared in the air to St. Francis, who was praying in a forest, and said to him: "Dost thou know me?"

"Who art thou?" asked the saint.

Said he: "I am that leper whom our Blessed Lord healed through thy merits, and today I am going to life eternal, for which I return thanks to God and to thee. Blessed be thy soul and thy body, blessed be thy holy words and works, for through thee many souls are saved in the world; and know that there is not a single day in which the angels and other saints do not return thanks to God for the holy fruits of thy preaching and that of thy Order in various parts of the world. Be comforted, then, and thank the Lord, and may His blessing rest on thee."

Having said these words, he went up to heaven, leaving St. Francis much consoled.

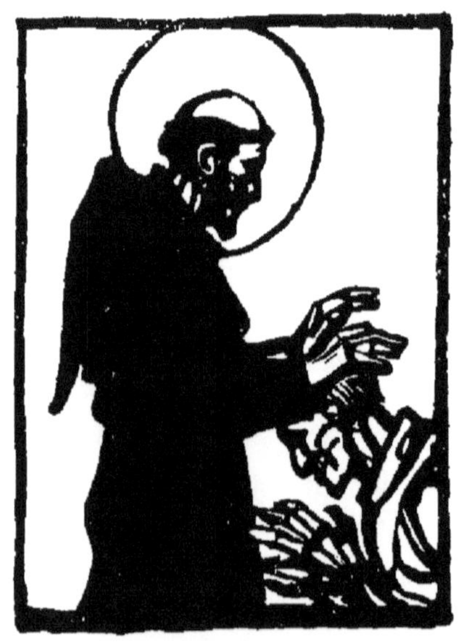

ROTHER BERNARD of Quintavalle was an example of the manifestation of the grace of God in the poor followers of the Gospel, who gave up the world to follow Christ. For since he had taken the habit of St. Francis, he was often rapt in God through the contemplation of celestial things.

It happened one day, as he was in a church hearing Mass, his mind was so raised to God that he was transfixed and enraptured, so as not to be aware of the moment of the elevation of the Body of Christ; for he neither knelt down nor removed his hood, as did the others, but remained motionless, with his eyes intently gazing upwards, and remained so even from Matins till the hour of None.

On coming back to himself, he went about the convent crying out with a loud voice: "O brothers! O brothers! O brothers! There is not a man in all this land, however great and however noble he may be, who, even if a palace full of gold were offered him, would not willingly carry on his back a sack of copper to acquire so rich a treasure."

Now this celestial treasure, promised to the lovers of Christ, had been revealed to Brother Bernard; and his mind was so fixed upon it, that for fifteen years his heart and countenance was raised away to heaven. In all that time he never satisfied his hunger, though he ate a little of whatever was set before him; wherefore he used to say that if a man does not taste what he eats his abstinence has no merit, for true abstinence is to moderate oneself in those things which are agreeable to the palate.

His intelligence also became so enlightened that many great divines had recourse to him to solve difficult questions and explain obscure passages of Scripture, which he did with great facility. So completely was his mind detached and withdrawn from all things earthly, that he soared like the swallows above the earth, and remained sometimes twenty, sometimes thirty days at the top of a high mountain contemplating things divine. For which reason Brother Giles said that he had received a gift from

God which had been given to no other human being—namely, that in his divine flight he was fed like the swallows.

And, because of this wonderful grace of contemplation which he had received from God, St. Francis willingly and frequently held converse with him day and night; and often they were found to be in a state of ecstasy all night long, in the wood where they used to meet together to talk on things divine.

 ROTHER RUFFINO, one of the most noble men of the city of Assisi, a companion of St. Francis and a man of great sanctity, was one day violently tempted in mind on the subject of predestination, so that he grew quite melancholy and sorrowful; for the devil put it into his heart that he was damned, and not of the number of those predestined to life eternal, making him believe that all he did in the Order was of no avail.

And this temptation increasing more and more, he had not the courage to reveal it to St. Francis, though he never ceased to pray and to fast: for the enemy of his soul added sorrow to sorrow, not only fighting inwardly but likewise outwardly, taking various forms in order better to deceive him.

One day he appeared to him under that of a crucifix, and said to him: "O Brother Ruffino, why dost thou inflict on thyself penance and prayer, as thou art not of the number of the predestinate to life eternal? Believe me—for I know whom I have chosen and predestined—and believe not the son of Peter Bernardoni if he tell thee the contrary; and do not take his advice in this matter, since neither he nor any man knows the truth but I, who am the Son of God. Know of a certainty that thou art of the number of the damned; and the son of Peter Bernardoni, thy father, and his father likewise, are damned, and whosoever followeth them is damned also."

On hearing these words, Brother Ruffino was so blinded by the spirit of darkness, that he lost all the faith and love he had felt for St. Francis hitherto, and would not even communicate to him what was passing within him.

But that which Brother Ruffino did not reveal to his saintly father was revealed to him by the Holy Spirit. When, therefore, the saint learned to what dangers his son was exposed, he sent to him Brother Masseo; but Brother Ruffino refused to listen to him, saying: "What have I to do with Brother Francis?"

And Brother Masseo, enlightened by the Spirit of God and knowing the deceits of the devil, answered: "O Brother Ruffino, thou knowest that St. Francis may be compared to an angel of God, who has made known the truth to many souls in the world, and through whom we have received the grace of God; wherefore I will at all events that thou come with us to him, for I clearly see that thou art deceived by the devil."

On hearing these words, Brother Ruffino arose and went to St. Francis; and the saint, perceiving him at a distance, cried out: "O Brother Ruffino, thou foolish one, whom hast thou believed?" Then coming up to him, he related to him one by one all the temptations, both internal and external, to which he had been exposed, showing him clearly that he who had appeared to him was the devil and not Christ, and that he was by no means to listen to his suggestions; but if he appeared to him again and said unto him "Thou art damned," he was to say to him these words: "Open thy mouth!" and by this sign he would clearly know that he was the devil and not Christ; for no sooner should the words be uttered than he would immediately disappear.

"Thou shouldst have known," added the saint, "with whom thou wast dealing, when he hardened thy heart against all that was good, for such is his special office; but Christ, the Blessed One, never hardens the heart of the faithful; for on the contrary, His office is to soften the heart of man, according to the words of the prophet: *I will take away from thee the heart of stone, and will give thee a heart of flesh.*"

Then Brother Ruffino, seeing that St. Francis was acquainted with all his temptations in the order they had come to him, was deeply touched by his exhortations, and beginning to weep bitterly, he humbly confessed his guilt in concealing from him his trouble. He was greatly consoled and comforted by the admonitions of his saintly father, which St. Francis ended by saying: "My son, go to confession, and give not up the practice of thine accustomed prayers; know of a certainty that this temptation will be to thee a source of great consolation and humility, as thou shalt shortly see."

Then Brother Ruffino returned to his cell in the wood; and as he was praying and weeping bitterly, the enemy approached, bearing in his exterior the semblance of Christ Himself. He thus addressed him: "O Brother Ruffino, did I not tell thee not to listen to the son of Peter Bernardoni, nor to weary thyself with prayer and fasting, inasmuch as thou art damned? What is the use of inflicting on thyself privations in this world, seeing thou hast no hope of salvation after death?"

And immediately Brother Ruffino said, "Open thy mouth!"—upon which the devil left him in so great rage and fury, that all Monte Subasio, which was close by, was shaken to the very foundation, and large stones rolled down the sides, knocking against each other as they fell, and producing a great fire in all the valley; and the noise they made was so terrible that St. Francis and all his companions went out to see what had taken place: and even to this day those large stones are to be seen lying in great confusion.

Then Brother Ruffino saw plainly that it was the devil who had deceived him, and returning to St. Francis he threw himself at his feet, acknowledging his fault. St. Francis comforted him with kind words, and sent him back to his cell full of consolation.

As he was praying there most devoutly, Christ, the Blessed One, appeared to him, and filling his soul with the fire of divine love, He thus addressed him: "Thou didst well, my son, to believe in St. Francis; for he who made thee so unhappy was the devil. But I am Christ, thy Master; and in order to prove to thee that I am He, I promise thee that thou shalt never again be troubled in this way."

Having said these words. He departed, leaving the brother so happy, and enjoying such peace and sweetness of spirit, with his mind so raised above the things of this world, that for a whole day and night he was rapt in God, and from that moment he had no doubts as to his salvation, and became quite a new man. Most willingly would he have re-mained day and night in prayer and in the contemplation of divine things, had he been permitted to do so. Wherefore St. Francis said of him that he had been canonized during his lifetime by Christ, and that, save in his presence, he would not hesitate to call him St. Ruffino, even though he were still on earth.

HOW SAINT FRANCIS WAS ACQUAINTED WITH THE SECRETS OF THE CONSCIENCES OF ALL HIS BRETHREN

S OUR LORD Jesus Christ says in His Gospel, *I know my sheep and mine know me,* so the holy St. Francis, like a good shepherd, knew, through divine revelation, all the merits and virtues of his companions, and also their defects and faults, and was enabled to deal with them according to their needs—humbling the proud and exalting the humble, rebuking vice and praising virtue—as we read in the wonderful revelations which were made to him by God with regard to his first children.

Amongst others, we are told that once St. Francis was with his companions in a convent talking of God, when Brother Ruffino was absent, being in contemplation in the forest; and, as the saint was conversing with them, Brother Ruffino passed by at some distance, whereon St. Francis asked them whom they believed to be the holiest soul in the world.

They answered immediately that they believed it to be St. Francis.

The saint reproved them, saying: "Beloved brothers, I am the most unworthy and the vilest of all men in the world; but see there Brother Ruffino, who is now coming out of the forest; the Lord has revealed to me that his soul is one of the three most holy on earth; and I tell you candidly, I should not hesitate to call him St. Ruffino even during his lifetime, his soul being full of grace, and sanctified and canonized in heaven by our Lord Jesus Christ." This opinion St. Francis never expressed in the presence of Brother Ruffino.

That he was equally acquainted with the defects of his brethren, we learn in the case of Brother Elias, whom he often reproved for his pride; and of Brother John della Cappella, to whom he foretold that he would hang himself; and of that brother who was seized by the devil as a punishment for his disobedience; and of many others whose defects and virtues were clearly revealed to him by Christ.

HOW BROTHER MASSEO OBTAINED FROM CHRIST THE VIRTUE OF HUMILITY

HE FIRST companions of St. Francis set themselves with all their might to follow holy poverty with regard to earthly things, and to acquire every other virtue, as the sure means of obtaining celestial and eternal riches. It happened, therefore, that one day, as they were assembled together to speak of things divine, one of them related the following example: "There was a man, a great friend of God, to whom had been given the grace of a life contemplative as well as active. He was at the same time so humble, that he looked upon himself as a very great sinner; and his humility was to him a means of sanctification, and confirmed him in the grace of God; for it caused him to increase in virtue, and saved him from falling into sin."

And Brother Masseo, hearing such wonderful things of humility, and knowing it to be one of the greatest treasures of life eternal, was so inflamed with a love and desire of this virtue of humility, that he lifted his eyes to heaven with much fervor, and made a vow and firm resolution never again to rejoice until he should feel the said virtue to be firmly established in his soul.

From that moment he was constantly shut up in his cell, macerating his body with fasts and vigils and prayers, weeping before the Lord, and earnestly imploring Him to grant him this virtue, without which he felt that he was only worthy of hell, and with which the friend of God of whom he had heard was so richly endowed.

Brother Masseo having passed several days in this state of mind, as he was entering the forest and asking the Lord, who willingly listens to the prayers of the humble, with cries and tears to grant him this divine virtue, he heard a voice from heaven, which called him twice: "Brother Masseo! Brother Masseo!"

And he, knowing in his spirit that it was the voice of Christ, answered: "My Lord."

Then Christ answered: "What wilt thou give in exchange for this virtue which thou askest for?"

And Brother Masseo answered: "Lord, I will willingly give the eyes out of my head."

Christ answered: "I grant thee the virtue, and command at the same time that thou keep thine eyes."

And having said these words, the voice was silent; and Brother Masseo was so filled with the grace of humility, that from thenceforward he was constantly rejoicing. And often when he was in prayer he was heard to utter a joyful sound, like the song of a bird, resembling "u-u-u," and his face bore a most holy and happy expression. With this he grew so humble that he esteemed himself less than all other men in the world.

And Brother James of Fallerone having asked him why in his joy he used always the same sound, he replied gaily, that when he found all good in one way, he saw no reason to change it.

HOW SAINT CLARE, BY ORDER OF THE POPE, BLESSED THE BREAD WHICH WAS ON THE TABLE, AND HOW ON EACH LOAF APPEARED THE SIGN OF THE HOLY CROSS

AINT CLARE, a most devout servant of the Cross of Christ, and one of the sweetest flowers of St. Francis, was so holy, that not only the Bishops and Cardinals but the Pope himself wished to see and hear her, and went often to visit her in person.

One day, the Holy Father, amongst others, went to her convent to hear her speak of things celestial; and having long reasoned together, St. Clare ordered the table to be laid and bread to be placed upon it, in order that the Holy Father might bless it. Their spiritual conclave being at an end, St. Clare, kneeling down with great reverence, begged him to bless the bread which had been placed on the table.

To whom the Holy Father answered: "Most faithful sister, I will that thou bless this bread by the sign of the cross to which thou hast devoted thyself."

St. Clare said: "Most holy Father, excuse me. I should indeed by worthy of reproof if I, a miserable woman, should presume to give such a blessing in the presence of the Vicar of Christ."

Then the Pope answered: "In order that such an act be not looked upon as presumptuous, but that it may bear on it the marks of obedience, I command thee, in the name of holy obedience, to make on this bread the sign of the cross, and to bless it in the name of God."

At this St. Clare, like a true daughter of obedience, blessed the loaves most devoutly, making over them the sign of the holy cross; and, wonderful to relate, on all those loaves appeared a cross, most clearly marked; and some of them were eaten, but the rest were put aside, in order to testify of the miracle. And the Holy Father, having seen the miracle, thanked God; and taking some of the bread, went away, leaving his blessing with Sister Clare.

At that time Sister Ortolana, mother of St. Clare, and Sister Agnes, her sister, were living together in the convent with St. Clare, both most virtuous women, full of the Holy Spirit, likewise many other nuns, to whom St. Francis sent a great number of sick persons, who were all healed by their prayers and by the sign of the most holy cross.

HOW SAINT LOUIS, KING OF FRANCE, WENT IN PERSON IN A PILGRIM'S GARB TO VISIT THE HOLY BROTHER GILES

AINT LOUIS, King of France, went on a pilgrimage to visit the sanctuaries in the world. And having heard of the fame of the sanctity of Brother Giles, who was one of the first companions of St. Francis, he determined in his heart to go and visit him in person; for which object he set out for Perugia, where the said brother then lived.

He arrived at the convent-gate as if he had been a poor unknown pilgrim, and asked with great importunity for Brother Giles, without telling the porter who it was who wished to see him; and the porter went to Brother Giles, and told him there was a pilgrim at the gate who asked for him. But the Lord having revealed to Brother Giles that the pilgrim was the King of France, he left his cell in haste, and ran to the gate without asking any questions. They both knelt down and embraced each other with

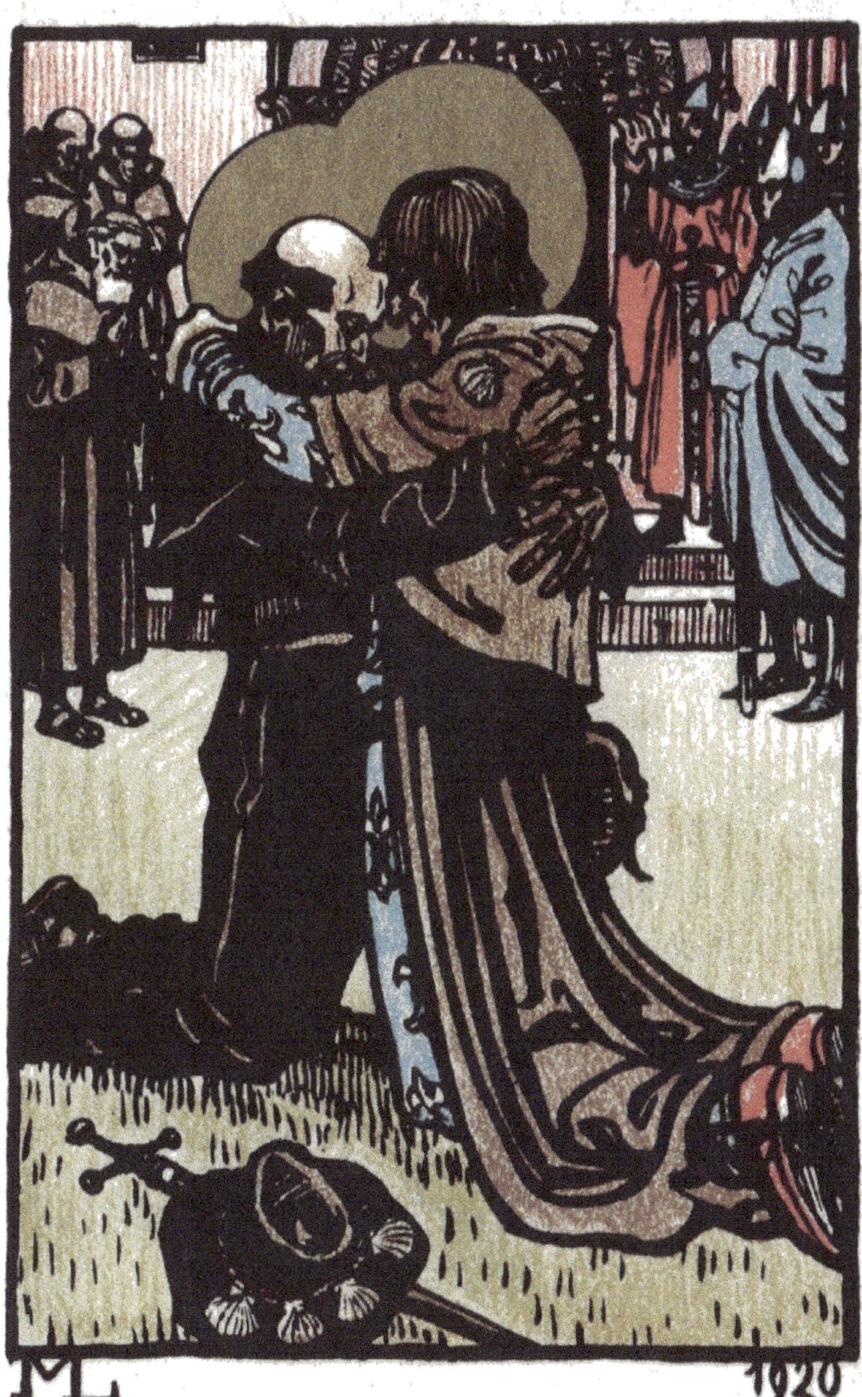

ML
1920

great reverence and many outward signs of love and charity, as if a long friendship had existed between them, though they had never met before in their lives. Neither of them spoke a word; and after remaining clasped in each other's arms for some time, they separated in silence, St. Louis to continue his journey, and Brother Giles to return to his cell.

As the king departed, a certain friar inquired of one of those who accompanied him who it was that had embraced Brother Giles, and he answered that it was Louis, King of France; and when the other brothers heard this, they were all sorrowful because Brother Giles had not spoken to him; and giving vent to their grief, they said: "O Brother Giles, why hast thou been so uncivil as not to say a word to so holy a king, who has come from France to see thee, and hear from thee some good words?"

Brother Giles answered: "Beloved brothers, be not surprised at this, that neither could I say a word to him nor he to me; for no sooner had we embraced each other than the light of divine wisdom revealed his heart to me, and mine to him; and by a divine operation we saw into each other's hearts, and knew far better what we had to say than if we had explained in words that which we felt in our hearts. For so imperfectly the tongue of man reveals the secret mysteries of God, that words would have been to us rather a hindrance than a consolation. Know, then, that the king went away from me well satisfied, and greatly comforted in mind."

HOW SAINT CLARE, BEING ILL, WAS MIRACULOUSLY CARRIED, ON CHRISTMAS NIGHT, TO THE CHURCH OF SAINT FRANCIS, WHERE SHE ASSISTED AT THE OFFICE

AINT CLARE was at one time so dangerously ill that she could not go to church with the other nuns to say the Office on the night of the Nativity of Christ. All the other sisters went to Matins; but she remained in bed, very sorrowful because she could not go with her sisters to receive spiritual consolation.

But Jesus Christ, her Spouse, unwilling to leave her comfortless, carried her miraculously to the church of St. Francis, so that she was present at Matins, assisted at the Midnight Mass, and received the Holy Communion, after which she was carried back to her bed.

When the nuns returned to their convent, the ceremonies being ended at St. Damiano, they went to St. Clare and said to her: "O Sister Clare, our Mother, what great consolations we have experienced at this feast of the Holy Nativity! Oh, if it had but pleased God that you should have been with us!"

To this St. Clare answered: "Praise and glory be to our Lord Jesus Christ, the Blessed One, my beloved sisters and daughters; for I have not only assisted at all the solemnities of this most holy night, but I have experienced in my soul even greater consolations than those which have been your share; for by the intercession of my father, St. Francis, and through the grace of our Savior Jesus Christ I have been personally present in the church of my venerable father, St. Francis, and with the ears of my body and those of my spirit have heard all the Office, and the sounds of the organ, and the singing, and have likewise received there the most Holy Communion. Rejoice, then, because of these graces which I have received, and return thanks to our Lord Jesus Christ."

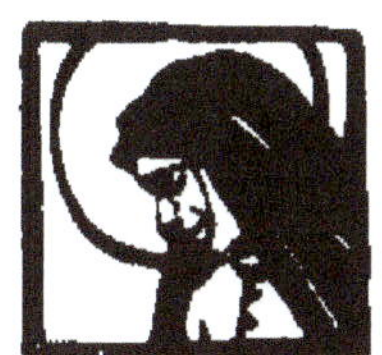

HOW SAINT FRANCIS EXPLAINED TO BROTHER LEO A BEAUTIFUL VISION THAT HE HAD SEEN

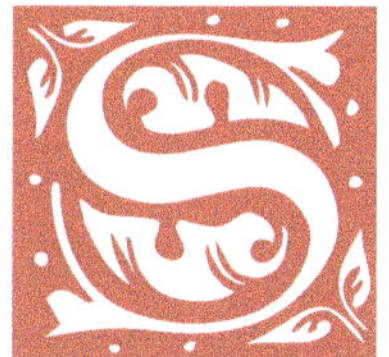

AINT FRANCIS being once grievously ill, Brother Leo, as he was in prayer by his bedside, was rapt in ecstasy, and carried in spirit to a great, wide and rapid river; and watching those who crossed it, he saw some brothers enter the river heavily laden, who were carried away by the current and were drowned; some contrived to reach one third of the way; others arrived as far as the middle of the stream; yet none could resist the rapidity of the waters, but fell down and were drowned. Presently he saw other brothers arrive; these carried nothing on their backs, but all bore upon themselves the marks of holy poverty. They entered the river, and passed over to the other side without any danger to themselves.

Having seen this, Brother Leo came to himself; and St. Francis knowing in spirit that he had had a vision, called him to him, and asked what he had seen. When Brother Leo had related to him the vision, St. Francis said: "What thou hast seen is indeed true. The great river is the world; the brothers who were drowned are those who do not follow their evangelical profession, or practice the great virtue of poverty; but they who passed the river are those who neither seek nor possess in this world any earthly riches, who having food and raiment are therewith content, and follow Christ naked on the cross, bearing joyfully and willingly His sweet and easy yoke and loving holy obedience: these pass easily from this earthly life to life eternal."

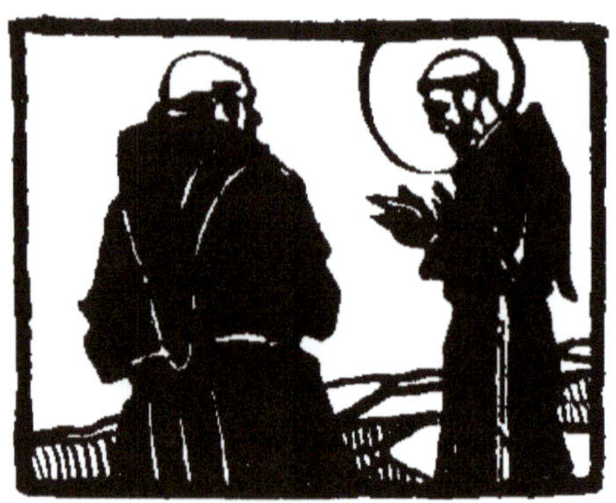

HOW JESUS CHRIST, THE BLESSED ONE, AT THE PRAYER OF SAINT FRANCIS, CONVERTED A RICH NOBLEMAN WHO HAD MADE GREAT OFFERS TO SAINT FRANCIS, AND INSPIRED HIM WITH A WISH TO BECOME A RELIGIOUS

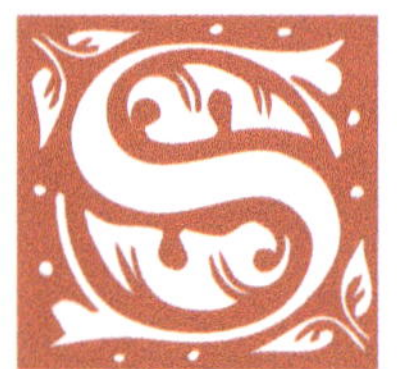

SAINT FRANCIS, the servant of Christ, arriving late one evening with one of his brothers at the house of a rich and powerful nobleman, the two were received by him as if they had been angels of God, with so much courtesy and respect that the saint felt himself drawn to love him greatly; for he considered how on entering his house he had embraced him with much affection; how he had washed his feet, and humbly wiped and kissed them; how he had lighted a great fire, and prepared a supper composed of the choicest meats, serving him himself with a joyful countenance.

When the supper was ended, the nobleman thus addressed St. Francis: "Behold, my father, I offer thee myself and all I possess. If ever thou art in want of a tunic, or a mantle, or any other thing, purchase them, and I will pay thee. And see, I am ready to provide for all thy wants, as, though the grace of God, it is in my power to do so; for I abound in all temporal riches, and out of love to God, who gave them to me, most willingly do I bestow my goods on His poor."

St. Francis, seeing so much courtesy and generosity, felt great affection towards him; and having taken leave of him, he said to his companion: "Truly this nobleman would be a great gain to our Order, seeing he is so grateful to God, and so kind and courteous to his neighbor and to the poor. For know, dear brother, that courtesy is one of the attributes of God, who sendeth His rain on the just and on the unjust; for courtesy is the sister of charity, it extinguisheth hatred and kindleth love. I have discovered in this good man such divine virtues, that I would most willingly have him as a companion. On some future day we will pay him another visit, for possibly the Lord may touch his heart, and induce him to follow us in his service; in the meantime we will pray God to put this desire into his heart, and give him grace to execute it."

Now a few days after St. Francis had made this prayer, the Lord touched the heart of the nobleman; and the saint said to his companion; "Let us go, my brother, to the dwelling of that courteous nobleman, as I hope in God that, amongst his temporal gifts, he will offer himself and join our Order"; and they set out accordingly.

As they arrived near the house, St. Francis said to his companion: "Wait for me a little, that I may first ask the Lord to prosper our journey, and pray that it may please our Savior Jesus Christ, through His holy Passion, to take from the world this virtuous nobleman, and confide him to us, His poor weak servants." Having said this, he knelt down in a spot where he could be seen by the nobleman, who was walking to and fro in his rooms; and it pleased God that he should perceive St. Francis as he prayed in the presence of Christ, who appeared in great glory and stood before him; he saw, too, that for a long space of time the saint was raised above the earth. On seeing this he felt in his heart so great a desire to leave the world, that he hastened out of his palace, and with great fervor of spirit ran to St. Francis, and kneeling at his feet implored him earnestly and devoutly to receive him into his Order, and allow him to do penance with him.

Then the saint, seeing that his prayer was granted, and that the nobleman asked of him the accomplishment of his wish, arose and embraced him joyfully, devoutly returning thanks to God, who had made such a present to his Order. And the nobleman said to St. Francis: "What wilt thou have me to do, my father? I am ready to obey thee, and give all I possess to the poor, in order to follow Christ with thee, without any hindrance from things temporal." And following the advice of the saint, he distributed all he possessed to the poor, and entered the Order, living a life of holiness and penance, and speaking always of divine things.

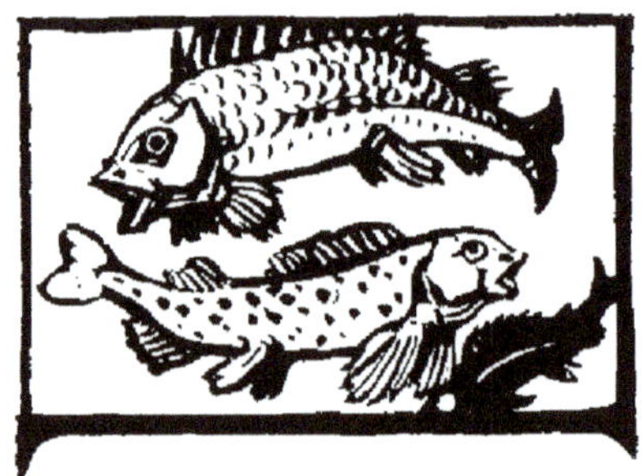

CHRIST, the Blessed One, was pleased to show forth the great sanctity of His most faithful servant St. Anthony, and how men ought devoutly to listen to his preaching, be means of creatures without reason. On one occasion, amongst others, he made use of fish to reprove the folly of faithless heretics: even as we read in the Old Testament that in ancient times he reproved the ignorance of Balaam by the mouth of an ass.

St. Anthony being at one time at Rimini, where there were a great number of heretics, and wishing to lead them by the light of faith into the way of truth, preached to them for several days, and reasoned with them on the faith of Christ and on the Holy Scriptures. They not only resisted his words, but were hardened and obstinate, refusing to listen to him.

At last St. Anthony, inspired by God, went down to the sea-shore, where the river runs into the sea, and having placed himself on a bank between the river and the sea, he began to speak to the fishes as if the Lord had sent him to preach to them, and said: "Listen to the word of God, O ye fishes of the sea and of the river, seeing that the faithless heretics refuse to do so."

No sooner had he spoken these words than suddenly so great a multitude of fishes, both small and great, approached the bank on which he stood, that never before had so many been seen in the sea or the river. All kept their heads out of the water, and seemed to be looking attentively on St. Anthony's face; all were ranged in perfect order and most peacefully, the smaller ones in front near the bank, after them came those a little bigger, and last of all, were the water was deeper, the largest.

When they had placed themselves in this order, St. Anthony began to preach to them most solemnly, saying: "My brothers the fishes, you are bound, as much as is in your power, to return thanks to your Creator, who has given you so noble an element for your dwelling; for you have at your choice both sweet water and salt; you have many places of refuge from the tempest; you have likewise a pure and transparent element for your nourishment. God, your bountiful and kind Creator, when He made you, ordered you to increase and multiply, and gave you His blessing. In the universal deluge, all other creatures perished; you alone did God preserve from all harm. He has given you fins to enable you to go where you will. To you was it granted, according to the commandment of God, to keep the prophet Jonas, and after three days to throw him safe and sound on dry land. You it was who gave the tribute-money to our Savior Jesus Christ, when, through His poverty, He had not wherewith to pay. By a singular mystery you were the nourishment of the eternal King, Jesus Christ, before and after His resurrection. Because of all these things you are bound to praise and bless the Lord, who has given you blessings so many and so much greater than to other creatures."

At these words the fish began to open their mouths, and bow their heads, endeavoring as much as was in their power to express their reverence and show forth their praise. St. Anthony, seeing the reverence of the fish towards their Creator, rejoiced greatly in spirit, and said with a loud voice: "Blessed be the eternal God; for the fishes of the sea honor Him more

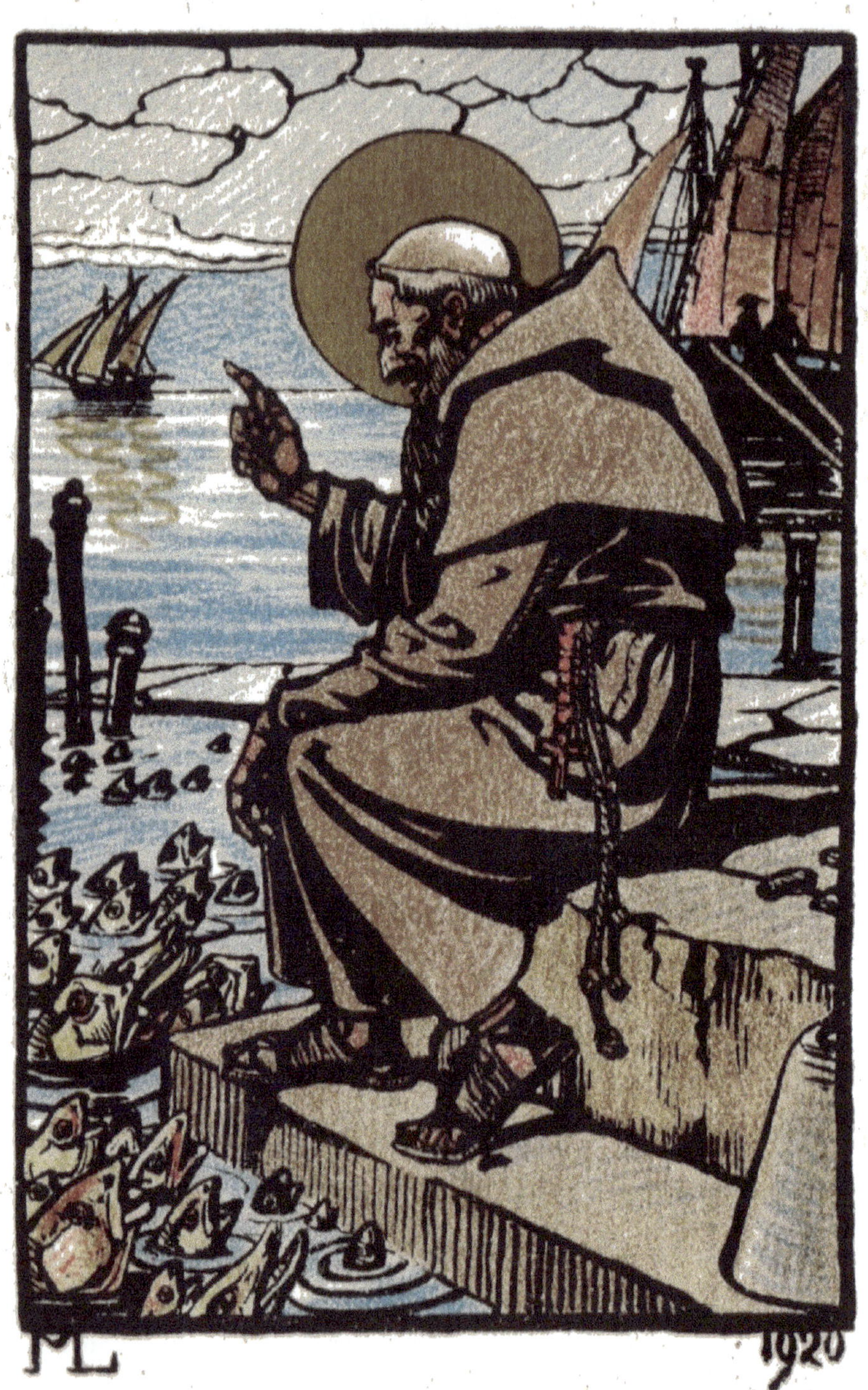
1920

than men without faith, and animals without reason listen to His word with greater attention than sinful heretics."

And whilst St. Anthony was preaching, the number of fishes increased, and none of them left the place that he had chosen. And the people of the city hearing of the miracle, made haste to go and witness it. With them also came the heretics of whom we have spoken above, who, seeing so wonderful and manifest a miracle, were touched in their hearts; and threw themselves at the feet of St. Anthony to hear his words. The saint then began to expound to them the Catholic faith. He preached so eloquently, that all those heretics were converted, and returned to the true faith of Christ; the faithful also were filled with joy, and greatly comforted, being strengthened in the faith.

After this St. Anthony sent away the fishes, with the blessing of God; and they all departed, rejoicing as they went, and the people returned to the city. But St. Anthony remained at Rimini for several days, preaching and reaping much spiritual fruit in the souls of his hearers.

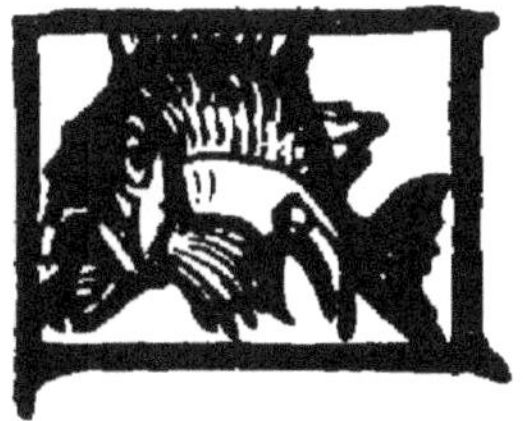

S THE SKY is adorned with stars, so the providence of the March of Ancona was in former times adorned with holy and exemplary friars, who, like the bright luminaries in heaven, ornamented the Order of St. Francis, and enlightened the world by their doctrine and example.

Foremost amongst these was Brother Lucido Antico, in whom indeed shone forth the fire of divine charity and the light of holiness; for, taught by the Spirit of God, his preaching produced innumerable fruits.

Another brother, Bentivoglio of Severino, was seen by Brother Masseo raised above the earth as he was praying in the forest, at the sight of which miracle Brother Masseo became a Friar Minor, and grew so holy that he worked many miracles, both during his lifetime and after his death: he is buried at Murro.

The said Brother Bentivoglio being once all alone at Trave Bonanti, nursing and serving a leper, received an order from his superior to go to another convent fifteen miles off. Not wishing to abandon the poor leper, he placed him carefully on his back, and charitably took him with him. Between the dawn of day and the rising of the sun he accomplished the fifteen miles, and arrived with his burden at the convent to which he had been sent, which was called Monte Sancino. Had he been an eagle he could not have flown as quickly, and such a miracle caused great wonder and surprise in all that country.

Another Brother, Peter of Monticello, who was the guardian of the old Convent of Ancona, was raised several feet above the earth, to the foot of the crucifix before which he was in prayer. This same Brother Peter having once observed the Lent of St. Michael with great devotion, as he was praying on the last day of the feast in the church, was heard to speak with St. Michael by a young man who had hidden himself behind the high altar, in hopes of seeing something wonderful; and the words which he heard were these.

The saint said to Brother Peter: "Thou hast suffered faithfully for my sake, and during many days hast mortified thy body; wherefore I am come to comfort thee, and whatever grace thou askest of God, I will obtain for thee."

Brother Peter answered: "Most holy prince of the celestial host of saints, faithful servant of divine love, and pious protector of souls, this is the grace I ask of thee, namely, that thou obtain from God the pardon of my sins."

And St. Michael answered: "Ask some other grace, as this I will most easily obtain." And as Brother Peter asked for nothing else, the Archangel added: "Through the faith and devotion which thou hast to me, I will obtain for thee not this grace only, but many others likewise." And when the conversation, which had lasted some time, was ended, the Archangel Michael departed, leaving Brother Peter greatly comforted.

At the same time lived Brother Conrad of Offida in the Convent of Forana in the custody of Ancona, where resided Brother Peter. Having gone one day into the forest to meditate on God, Brother Peter followed him to see what would befall him; and Brother Conrad began to implore the Virgin Mary, with great fervor and devotion, to obtain from her Blessed Son that he might experience somewhat of the sweetness which St. Simeon experienced the day of the Purification, when in his arms he held Jesus the Blessed Savior.

Having finished his prayer, the Virgin Mary obtained his request; and, behold!, the Queen of Heaven appeared in great splendor, with her Blessed Son in her arms, and approaching Brother Conrad placed the Holy Child in his arms. He received Him most reverently, and embracing Him clasped Him to his breast, his heart overflowing and burning with divine love and inexpressible consolation. Brother Peter, who witnessed this scene at a distance, felt likewise in his soul great sweetness and joy.

When the Virgin Mary had departed from Brother Conrad, Brother Peter hastened back to the convent that he might not be seen; but when Brother Conrad arrived, full of joy and happiness, Brother Peter said to him: "O brother, thou hast received great consolation today!"

And Brother Conrad answered: "What sayest thou, Brother Peter? How dost thou know? Hast thou seen me?"

"I know," answered Brother Peter, "that the Virgin Mary, with her Blessed Son, has visited thee." And Brother Conrad, who, through great humility, wished to keep secret the grace with which God had favored him, entreated Brother Peter to tell no one what he had witnessed; and from henceforth so great was the love which existed between these two brethren, that they seemed to have but one soul and one heart in all things.

The said Brother Conrad, being once in the Convent of Siruolo, delivered a woman who was possessed by a devil, by praying for her a whole night; and her mother coming to know it, he left the place in the morning, that he might not be discovered and honored by the people.

HOW BROTHER CONRAD OF OFFIDA CONVERTED A YOUNG BROTHER, WHO WAS A STUMBLING BLOCK TO THE OTHER BROTHERS, AND HOW AFTER DEATH HIS SOUL APPEARED TO BROTHER CONRAD, BEGGING HIM TO PRAY FOR HIM, AND HOW THROUGH HIS PRAYER HE WAS DELIVERED FROM THE GREAT PAINS OF PURGATORY

HE LIFE of the said Brother Conrad of Offida, the great advocate of evangelical poverty and of the Rule of St. Francis, was so exemplary and so meritorious in the sight of God, that Christ, the Blessed One, honored him with many miracles, not only after death, but likewise during his life.

Amongst others, being once on a visit to the Convent of Offida, the brothers begged him, for the love of God and of holy charity, to reprove a young brother in the said convent, whose conduct was so puerile and disordered, and his manners so dissolute, that he distracted all the brethren, both young and old, at divine office, and cared little or nothing for any of the observances of religious life.

At the request of the brothers, and out of compassion for the said young man, Brother Conrad called him to him one day, and reproved him with so much charity, that a complete change took place in his heart, and the said young man, putting off his former childish way of life, became so obedient, so meek, so devout, so anxious to do what was right, so ready to serve others, and so zealous in the practice of every virtue, that the brethren, to whom he had hitherto been a stumbling block, found in him much comfort and satisfaction, so that they loved him dearly.

Shortly after this conversion it pleased God to take him out of the world; and his death caused great sorrow to the brethren.

A few days after his soul had left the body, it appeared to Brother Conrad as he was in prayer before the altar of the convent, devoutly saluting him as his father. On Brother Conrad asking who he was, he answered: "I am the soul of the young brother who died a few days ago."

Said Brother Conrad to him: "My beloved son, how is it with thee?"

And the soul answered: "By the grace of God, and through thy teaching, I have cause to be thankful, for I am not damned; but because of certain sins of which I had not time to repent while I was in the world, I am suffering the extremist pain of purgatory; and I pray thee, Father, as thou hadst compassion on me when living, to help me now by thy prayers, and say for me some Paters, for thy prayers are most acceptable to God."

Then Brother Conrad, continuing his devotions, said for him a *Pater* with a *Requiem aeternam.*

At this the soul said: "Holy Father, I am greatly refreshed already, and I pray thee to repeat thy prayer for me."

Brother Conrad did as he was begged, and the soul said again: "As thou prayest for me, my sufferings are relieved; wherefore I implore thee, cease not to pray for me."

Then Brother Conrad, seeing that the soul of the young man was relieved by his prayers, said for his intention a hundred *Paters*; and when they were finished of soul said to him: "I thank thee, dearest Father, in the name of God, for thy great charity towards me; through thy prayers I have been delivered from the pains of purgatory, and am going to heaven," and with this the soul departed.

Brother Conrad, in order to comfort and console the brethren, related to them the vision. And on this wise the soul of the young brother went to heaven, through the merits of Brother Conrad.

HEN BROTHER CONRAD and the aforenamed Brother
Peter, the two shining lights of the custody of Ancona,
were living together in the Convent of Forano, such love
and charity existed between them that they seemed to
have but one heart and one soul; and they would make
known to each other and share every mercy which the Lord should send
them.

Having made this agreement, it happened one day, as Brother Peter
was praying, devoutly meditating on the Passion of Christ, and how His
Blessed Mother, with St. John the Evangelist and St. Francis, were repre-
sented at the foot of the cross, as having been crucified with Christ in
mental sufferings, he felt a great wish to know which of the three had suffered the greatest sorrow on account of the Passion of Christ—the Mother who had given Him birth, the disciple who had laid his head on His
bosom, or St. Francis, who was, as it were, crucified with Him.

As he was meditating on this, the Virgin Mary appeared to him,
with St. John the Evangelist and St. Francis, all clothed in the heavenly
garb of glorified souls; and St. Francis seemed to be dressed more richly
than St. John. At this vision Brother Peter was greatly terrified, but St.
John comforted him by saying: "Fear not, dear brother; for we are come
to enlighten thee in thy doubt: know, then, that the Mother of Christ, and
I, His disciple, have suffered above every other creature at His Passion,
and after us St. Francis has suffered more than all others, and this is why
thou seest him in such glory."

And Brother Peter said: "Why then, most holy Apostle of Christ,
are the vestments of St. Francis more beautiful than thine?"

"Because," answered St. John, "when he was in the world, he wore a
humbler dress than I."

And having said these words, he gave to Brother Peter a glorious
vestment that he had in his hand, saying: "Take this dress which I have
brought for thee." Then St. John being about to put it on him, Brother

Peter fell down in terror, and began to cry out: "Brother Conrad, Brother Conrad, haste thou to help me! come and see most wonderful things!" And as he said these words, the vision disappeared.

Then Brother Peter related to Brother Conrad all he had seen, and they together returned thanks to God.

OF A HOLY BROTHER TO WHOM THE MOTHER OF CHRIST APPEARED

IN THE ABOVE-MENTIONED Convent of Soffiano there lived formerly a Friar Minor so holy that he appeared to be almost supernatural, and he was often rapt in God. He possessed the grace of contemplation in a notable degree; and often when he was ravished and raised above the earth in ecstasy, all kinds of birds used to come and perch on his head, his arms, and his hands, singing most wonderfully. He was very fond of solitude, and rarely spoke; but when anyone asked him a question he answered so wisely and so graciously that he seemed to be an angel rather than a mortal. He was a man wholly devoted to prayer and contemplation, and the brothers held him in great reverence.

Having finished the course of his virtuous life, it was the will of God that he should fall dangerously ill, so that he could take no nourishment, and he refused all human remedies, placing all his hope in the celestial Physician, Jesus Christ, the Blessed One, and His divine Mother, by whom, through the mercy of God, he was visited and healed. For as he was lying on his bed, preparing for death with all his heart and with great devotion, the glorious Virgin Mary, Mother of Christ, appeared to him with a great multitude of angels and holy virgins, and surrounded by much splendor. She approached his bed, and on seeing her, he experienced the greatest comfort and joy both in soul and body, and began to pray to her humbly, to ask of her divine Son to deliver his soul from its miserable prison of flesh.

As he persevered in prayer, with many tears, the Virgin Mary called him by his name, saying to him: "My son, have no doubts; for thy prayer is granted, and I am come to comfort thee a little before thou leavest this world."

By the side of the Virgin Mary there stood three holy virgins, holding in their hands three vases filled with a sweet ointment; and the Virgin Mary taking one of the vases opened it, when all the house was filled with the odour thereof; then taking a spoonful of the contents she gave it to the sick brother. No sooner had he tasted it than he experienced so sweet a sensation, that it seemed as if his soul could no longer remain in his body, and he cried out: "No more, O blessed Virgin Mary; no more, O blessed Physician, whose pleasure it is to save the human race from perishing; I cannot endure such sweetness." But the compassionate Mother of God continued to give him the ointment, until the vase was emptied.

The first vase being emptied, the Blessed Virgin took the second, and was about to give him the contents; but he said: "O blessed Mother of God, if my soul is, as it were, melted by the sweetness and virtue of the ointment thou hast already given me, how shall I ever be able to support the effect of a second vase: I pray thee, O Virgin, blessed above all the saints and all the angels, not to give me any more." The glorious Virgin Mary answered: "Taste, my son, a little of the second vase"; and having given him a little, she said: "Thou has sufficient, my son, for today; soon I will come again to conduct thee to the kingdom of my Son, Whom thou hast ever sought and desired"; and having said these words, she took leave of him and departed.

And the brother was so strengthened and comforted by the medicine she had given him, that he lived for several days in perfect health, without taking any nourishment. Shortly after, as he was talking gaily with the brethren, he passed from this miserable life most joyfully.

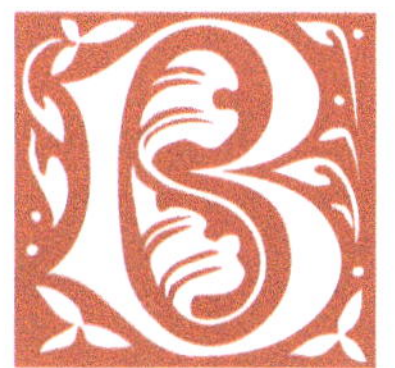ROTHER JAMES della Massa, to whom the Lord revealed many secrets, and to whom He gave a perfect knowledge of the Holy Scriptures and of the future, was so holy, that Brother Giles of Assisi, Brother Mark of Montino, Brother Juniper, and Brother Lucido said of him that they knew no one in the world who was greater in the sight of God than this Brother James.

I had a great wish to see him; for having asked Brother John, the companion of Brother Giles, to explain to me certain spiritual things, he said to me: "If thou wilt be well directed in things spiritual, try to speak with Brother James della Massa; for his words being the words of the Holy Spirit, one can neither add to nor take away from them anything, and there is not a man on earth whom I have a greater wish to see."

When Brother John of Parma was a minister of the convent, this Brother James was once, in prayer, ravished in God, remaining for three days in ecstasy, quite insensible to all bodily feeling, so that the brethren thought him to be dead; and during this ecstasy many things with regard to the Order were revealed to him. Having learnt this, my wish to speak to him and to hear him greatly increased.

When the Lord permitted me to see him, I thus addressed him: "If that which I have heard of thee be true, I pray thee not to conceal it from me. I have heard that when thou wast three days as if thou hadst been dead, the Lord revealed to thee, amongst other things, what was to take place in our Order; and this was told me by Brother Matthew, to whom thou didst reveal it out of obedience." Brother James confessed most humbly that what Brother Matthew had said was true.

Now this is what Brother Matthew told me: "I know a brother to whom the Lord has made known that which will take place in our Order; for Brother James della Massa had told me that, after the Lord had revealed to him many things concerning the Church militant, he saw in a vision a large and beautiful tree, the root of which was of gold, and all the branches were men, and these men were all Friars Minor; and there were as many large branches as there were provinces in the Order, and each branch was composed of as many brethren as there were friars in each province; and he was informed of the number of friars in the Order, and in each province—with their names, their ages, their rank, and the different offices they filled—also their various merits and defects.

"And he saw Brother John of Parma at the summit of the highest branch of the tree, and round him were the ministers of each province; and he saw Christ, the Blessed One, sitting on a throne, who, calling St. Francis to Him, gave him a chalice full of the spirit of life, saying, 'Go to thy brothers, and give them to drink of this spirit of life, as Satan will rise up against them, and many will fall and not rise again.' And Christ, the Blessed One, gave to St. Francis two angels to accompany him; and St. Francis took the chalice to his brothers, and offered it first to Brother John of Parma, who taking it drank all its contents in haste, but with great reverence, and having done so he became luminous, like the sun.

"After him St. Francis offered it to all the others; and very few there were who took it, and drank with devotion: those who did so, were filled with light, like the sun; but those who took the chalice, and threw away its contents most irreverently, became black and deformed, and horrible to look at; those who drank a part of the contents and threw away the rest, were partly bright and partly dark, in proportion to the quantity they drank or threw away. The brightest of all was the said Brother John, who, having drained to the dregs the cup of life, had seen by the aid of a celestial light the tempests and troubles which were about to rise against the tree, shaking and tearing its branches; for which reason the said Brother John left the top of the tree where he was, and placing himself under its branches hid himself close to the roots.

"A brother who had drunk some and thrown away some of the contents of the chalice, took possession of the place on the branch he had left; no sooner was he there, than the nails of his fingers became like points of iron; on seeing this, he hastened to leave the place he had taken, and in his fury he sought to vent his rage on Brother John; and Brother John perceiving his intention, cried out to Christ, the Blessed One, who was seated on His throne, to help him; and Christ, hearing his cry, called St. Francis, and giving him a sharp stone, said: 'Take this stone, and going cut the nails of the brother who seeks to tear Brother John, so that he may not be able to do him any harm.' And St. Francis did as he was ordered.

"In the meantime a great tempest arose and the wind shook the tree in such a way that all the brethren fell to the ground. First fell those who had thrown away the contents of the chalice of the spirit of life: these were carried by devils to dark regions, full of pain and anguish; but Brother John, and others who had drunk of the chalice, were carried by angels to the regions of life eternal, full of light and splendor. And Brother James, who witnessed the vision, saw clearly the names, the condition and the fate of each brother. And the tempest did not cease till the tree was blown down, and carried away by the wind; and immediately another tree arose out of the golden roots of the old one, and it was entirely composed of gold, with its leaves and fruits; but for the present we will not describe the beauty, the virtues, and the delicious fragrance of this wonderful tree."

HOW CHRIST APPEARED TO BROTHER JOHN OF ALVERNIA

MONG the learned and holy brethren and sons of St. Francis, who, as Solomon says, form the glory of their Father, was the venerable and holy Brother John of Fermo, of the province of Ancona, who lived in our times. Having spent the greater part of his life in the holy house of Alvernia, he died there, and was known by the name of Brother John of Alvernia; he was man of great holiness and great sanctity.

This Brother John, when he was a child, greatly loved the ways of penance, which preserve the purity both of the body and of the soul; and at a very tender age he began to wear a belt of iron, and to observe great fasting and abstinence; more especially he used these mortifications when he was residing with the Canons of San Pietro di Fermo, who lived in great luxury; he avoided all pleasures, and macerated his body with great severity. His companions, being against such penitential ways, tried by every means to turn him from them, taking from him his instruments of penance, and preventing him from fasting; wherefore the holy child, inspired by God, resolved to leave the world and its worshippers, and to put himself in the arms of his crucified Lord, taking the habit of the crucified St. Francis; which he did.

Being received into the Order so young, and confided to the care of the master of the novices, he grew so spiritual and so devout, that whenever he heard the said master speak of God, he felt his heart to burn within him, as if it had been on fire, so that it was impossible for him to remain quiet, and he ran to and fro in the garden, in the forest, and even in the church; for so sweet was the sensation he experienced, that it seemed to him as if his heart was melted like wax before the fire.

As time went on, this holy youth advanced from virtue to virtue, and his soul was adorned and enriched with spiritual gifts; he was often rapt in ecstasy, so that his mind was raised at times to the splendors of the cherubim, at times to the ardor of the seraphim and the joys of the beatified. At one time this ecstasy of divine love, which seemed, as it were, to set his heart on fire, lasted for three years, and this took place on the holy mountain of Alvernia.

But as God takes special care of his children, sending them at diverse times consolation or tribulation, adversity or prosperity, according to their need, in order to preserve in them the grace of humility, or to awaken in their hearts a greater thirst after spiritual things, so it pleased His divine bounty, when the three years were ended, to withdraw from Brother John this flame of celestial love, and take from him every spiritual consolation. Then was Brother John most disconsolate and sorrowful and this great trial made him so miserable, that he wandered about the forest, crying out with sighs and tears for the beloved Spouse of his soul, for without His presence his soul could enjoy neither peace nor rest. Yet nowhere could he find his Beloved, or recover those sweet spiritual sensations to which the love of Christ had accustomed him.

Now this trial lasted several days, during which time he persevered in prayer, weeping and sighing, and imploring the Lord to take pity on His soul, and restore to him his Beloved. At last, his patience having been sufficiently tried, as he was wandering one day sorrowfully in the forest he sat down, overcome with fatigue; and as he was gazing up to heaven, with his eyes full of tears, Jesus Christ, the Blessed One, appeared to him, standing in silence on the path by which he himself had come.

Brother John knew Him to be the Christ, and throwing himself at His feet he burst into a flood of tears, and thus addressed Him: "Help me, O my Lord! for without Thee, my sweet Savior, I am all in sorrow and in darkness; without Thee, gentle Lamb, I am in anguish and fear; without Thee, Son of the Most High God, I am in confusion and in shame; without Thee, I am despoiled of every good, for Thou art Jesus Christ, the true light of my soul; without Thee, I am lost and damned, for Thou art the life of souls, the life of life; without Thee, I am sterile and unfruitful, for Thou art the foundation of every grace; without Thee, I can have no consolation, for Thou, O Jesus, art our Redeemer, our love, our desire, the bread of comfort, the wine which rejoices the hearts of angels and of saints; enlighten me, O pitying Shepherd, for I am Thy lamb, albeit most unworthy."

When the Lord delays to grant the desires of holy men, their love towards Him greatly increaseth; for the which reason Christ, the Blessed One, left Brother John, going from him without granting his request, and without speaking to him.

Then Brother John arose, and running after Him threw himself again at his feet, imploring Him not to leave him, and crying out: "O Jesus Christ, most sweet Savior, have mercy on me in my trouble; by the truth of Thy salvation and the multitude of Thy mercies, restore to me the joy of Thy countenance, and cast upon me a look of pity; for the earth is full of Thy mercy"; but the Lord Jesus went from him without saying a word, or leaving him any consolation.

Then Brother John followed Him with great fervor, and when he came up to Him, Christ, the Blessed One, turned round, and looking at him most sweetly, He opened His holy and merciful arms and embraced him; and when He opened His arms Brother John saw rays of light come from His holy bosom, which lighted up all the forest, as well as his own soul and body. Then Brother John knelt down at the feet of Christ, the Blessed One, Who, as He had given His foot to Mary Magdalene to kiss, so now gave He it to Brother John. Then Brother John, taking it with great reverence, bathed it with his tears like another Magdalene, saying most devoutly, "I pray Thee, my Lord, look not at my sins, but, by Thy holy Passion and by the precious Blood which Thou hast shed, awaken my soul to the grace of Thy love; for Thou hast commanded us to love

Thee with all our heart and with all our strength; which commandment none can fulfill without Thy help. Help me, then, beloved Son of God, that I may love Thee with all my heart and all my strength."

And as Brother John was thus praying at the feet of Christ, his prayer was granted, and the flame of divine love which he had lost was restored to him, and he felt himself greatly comforted. Then knowing that the gift of divine grace had been restored to him, he began to return thanks to Christ, the Blessed One, and devoutly to kiss His feet. Then standing up, and looking on the Savior's face, Jesus Christ gave him His holy hands to kiss; and having kissed them, Brother John approached the bosom of Christ, and embraced Him. Christ, the Blessed One, received him in His arms; and as Brother John embraced the Savior, and was embraced by Him, the air was filled with the sweetest perfumes, so sweet that no other perfume in the world could be compared with them.

Thus was Brother John consoled, enlightened, and rapt in ecstasy, and this sweet perfume lasted in his soul for many months; and thenceforth from his lips, which had drunk at the fountain of divine wisdom on the sacred bosom of the Savior, there fell most wonderful and celestial words, which changed the hearts of those who heard them, producing great fruit in souls; and for a long time, whenever Brother John followed the path in the forest where the blessed feet of Christ had passed, he saw the same wonderful light and breathed the same sweet odor.

When Brother John came back to himself after this vision, though the corporal presence of Christ had disappeared, his mind was so enlightened and so imbued with divine wisdom, that although he was not a learned man or versed in human studies, he explained most wonderfully the most difficult questions on the Holy Trinity and the profound mysteries of Holy Writ; and when speaking before the Pope, the cardinals, the king, the barons, the masters, and doctors, they were surprised at his sublime discourse, and at the words of wisdom which he pronounced.

HOW BROTHER JOHN OF ALVERNIA, WHEN SAYING MASS ON THE DAY OF ALL SOULS, SAW MANY SOULS LIBERATED FROM PURGATORY

S BROTHER JOHN was saying Mass on the day after All Saints, for the souls of the dead, as the Church has ordered, he offered with such charity and such compassion the Holy Sacrifice, which the dead desire above all else we can give them, that he seemed to be overwhelmed and consumed by the ardor of the feelings which filled his heart; and when he lifted up the Body of Christ and devoutly offered It to God the Father, entreating Him, for the love of His blessed Son Jesus Christ, who had died on the cross for the souls of men, to deliver from the pains of purgatory the souls of the dead which He had created and redeemed, he saw immediately an immense number of souls go out from purgatory, like innumerable sparks of fire coming out of a burning oven; and he saw them go up to heaven, through the merits of the Passion of Christ, who is daily offered for the living and the dead in that most Holy Sacrifice, which is worthy to be adored for ever and ever.

HOW, WHILE HE WAS SAYING MASS, BROTHER JOHN OF ALVERNIA FELL DOWN, AS IF HE HAD BEEN DEAD

MOST WONDERFUL thing befell the said Brother John in the above-mentioned Convent of Moliano, as is related by the brethren who were present. The first night after the Octave of St. Lawrence, and within the Octave of the Assumption of our Lady, having said Matins in the church with the other brethren, the unction of God's grace coming upon him, he went into the garden to meditate on the Passion of Christ, and prepare himself most devoutly to celebrate Mass, which it was his turn to sing that morning.

As he was meditating on the words of the Consecration of the Body of Christ and contemplating the boundless charity of Jesus, who not only bought us with His precious Blood, but left His Body and His Blood as food for our souls, the love of sweet Jesus so filled his heart that he could not contain himself, and cried out several times, *Hoc est Corpus meum.* As he said these words Christ, the Blessed One, appeared to him, with the Virgin Mary and a multitude of angels, and the Spirit of God made knows to him high mysteries of that great sacrament.

When day dawned he entered the church, so absorbed by all he had seen that he repeated aloud the above words, with great fervor of spirit, believing that he was not seen or heard by any one (but there was a brother praying in the choir who saw and heard everything), and he remained in this state till the hour came to say Mass.

He approached the altar, and began the sacrifice; as he proceeded, his heart so overflowed with love to Christ, and the sensation he experienced was so ineffable, that he could not express it in words, and he was in doubt whether he ought to leave off the celebration of Mass or to go on. The same thing having happened to him before, and the Lord having moderated the sensation, so that he was enabled to finish the sacrifice, trusting that he would do so again, he proceeded, with great fear and trembling.

When he arrived at the Preface of our Lady, the divine illumination and the sensation of ardent love towards God so increased in his heart, that when he reached the *Qui pridie* he could scarcely resist any longer. When he came to the Consecration, and had pronounced over the host half of the words, that is to say, *Hoc est,* it was quite impossible for him to go on, but he repeated over and over the same words, *Hoc est enim;* and the reason why he could not proceed was that he saw before him Christ Himself, with a multitude of angels, and he could not endure His Majesty. He saw that Christ would not enter the host, nor would it be changed into the Body of Christ, unless he pronounced the other words of the Consecration, namely, *Corpus meum.*

Being greatly perplexed and unable to go on, the guardian, with the other brothers, and the people who were in the church to hear Mass, approached the altar and stood amazed, seeing and considering the actions of Brother John; and many were moved to tears by his devotion.

At last, after a long time, it pleased God that Brother John should pronounce in a loud voice the words, *enim Corpus meum;* and immediately the form of bread was changed, and Jesus Christ, the Blessed One, appeared in the host, in His bodily shape, and in great glory, showing thereby the humility and charity which made Him to take flesh of the Virgin Mary, and which now places Him daily in the hands of the priest when he consecrates the host. By this Brother John was raised to a state of contemplation yet sweeter, insomuch that, when he had elevated the host and the consecrated chalice, he was ravished out of himself, and all corporal sensations being suspended, his body fell back. If he had not been supported by the guardian, who was behind him, he would have fallen to the ground; and all the friars with the men and women who were in the church gathering round him, he was carried to the sacristy as if dead, for his body was quite cold, and his fingers so stiffened that they could neither be opened nor moved; and in this state he remained till the third hour, as it was summer.

When he came back to himself, I, who was present, feeling a great desire to know what he had experienced, went to him, and begged him, for the love of God, to tell me everything. As he greatly trusted me, he related all that had happened to him; and amongst other things, he told me that, as he was consecrating the Body and Blood of Christ, his soul seemed to melt within him like wax, and his body to be without bones, so that he could not lift his arms or his hands, or make the sign of the cross on the host or on the chalice. He told me likewise that, before he became a priest, it had been revealed to him by God that he should faint away when saying Mass; but having said many Masses, and no such thing having yet happened to him, he thought that the revelation did not come from God. Nevertheless, about fifty days before the Assumption of our Lady, when this thing befell him, it had been again revealed to him by God that it should so happen to him about the time of the Feast of the Assumption: but this vision or revelation from our Lord he did not call to mind at the moment.

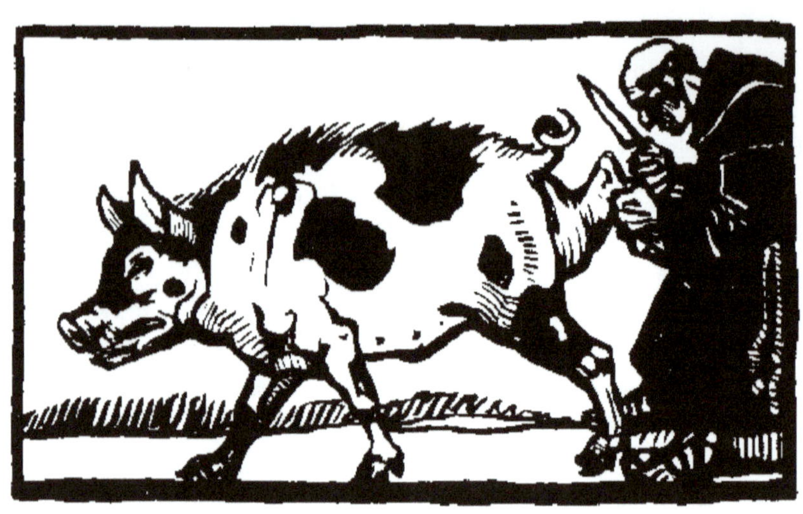

HOW BROTHER JUNIPER CUT OFF THE FOOT OF A PIG TO GIVE IT TO A SICK BROTHER

NE of the most chosen disciples and first companions of St. Francis was Brother Juniper, a man of profound humility and of great fervor and charity, of whom St. Francis once said, when speaking of him to some of his companions: "He would be a good Friar Minor who had overcome the world as perfectly as Brother Juniper."

Once when he was visiting a sick brother at St. Mary of the Angels, he said to him, as if all on fire with the charity of God: "Can I do thee any service?" And the sick man answered: "Thou wouldst give me great consolation if thou couldst get me a pig's foot to eat."

Brother Juniper answered immediately: "Leave it to me; thou shalt have one at once." So he went and took a knife from the kitchen, and in fervor of spirit went into the forest, where many swine were feeding, and having caught one, he cut off one of its feet and ran off with it, leaving the swine with its foot cut off; and coming back to the convent, he carefully washed the foot, and diligently prepared and cooked it. Then he brought it with great charity to the sick man, who ate it with avidity; and Brother Juniper was filled with joy and consolation, and related the history of his assault upon the swine for his diversion.

Meanwhile, the swineherd who had seen the brother cut off the foot, went and told the tale in order, and with great bitterness, to his lord, who, being informed of the fact, came to the convent and abused the friars, calling them hypocrites, deceiver, robbers, and evil men. "Why," said he, "have you cut off the foot of my swine?" At the noise which he made, St. Francis and all the friars came together, and with all humility made excuses for their brother, and, as ignorant of the fact, promised, in order to appease the angry man, to make amends for the wrong which had been done to him.

But he was not to be appeased, and left St. Francis with many threats and reproaches, repeating over and over again that they had maliciously cut the foot off his swine, refusing to accept any excuse or promise of repayment; and so departed in great wrath. And as all the other friars wondered: "Can Brother Juniper indeed have done this through indiscreet zeal?," he sent for him, and asked him privately: "Hast thou cut off the foot of a swine in the forest?"

To which Father Juniper answered quite joyfully, not as one who has committed a fault, but believing he had done a great act of charity: "It is true, sweet Father, that I did cut off that swine's foot; and if thou wilt listen compassionately, I will tell thee the reason. I went out of charity to visit the brother who is sick." And so he related the matter in order, adding: "I tell thee, dear father, that this foot did the sick brother so much good, that if I had cut off the feet of a hundred swine instead of one, I verily believe that God would have been pleased therewith."

To whom St. Francis, in great zeal for justice, and in much bitterness of heart, made answer: "O Brother Juniper, wherefore hast thou given this great scandal? Not without reason doth this man complain, and thus rage against us; perhaps even now he is going about the city spreading this evil report of us, and with good cause. Therefore I command thee by holy obedience, that thou go after him until thou find him, and cast thyself prostrate before him, confessing thy fault, and promising to make such full satisfaction that he shall have no more reason to complain of us, for this is indeed a most grievous offence."

At these words Brother Juniper was much amazed, wondering that any one should have been angered at so charitable an action, for all temporal things appeared to him of no value, save in so far as they could be charitably applied to the service of our neighbor. So he made answer: "Doubt not, Father, but that I shall soon content and satisfy him. And why should there be all this disturbance, seeing that the swine was rather God's than his, and that it furnished the means for an act of charity?"

And so he went his way, and coming to the man, who was still chafing and past all patience, he told him for what reason he had cut off the pig's foot, and all with such fervor, exultation and joy, as if he were telling him of some great benefit he had done him which deserved to be highly rewarded.

The man grew more and more furious at his discourse, and loaded him with much abuse, calling him a fantastical fool and a wicked thief. Brother Juniper, who delighted in insults, cared nothing for all this abuse, but marveling that any one should be wroth at what seemed to him only a matter of rejoicing, he thought he had not made himself well understood, and so repeated the story all over again, and then flung himself on the man's neck and embraced him, telling him that all had been done out of charity, and inciting and begging him for the same motive to give the rest of the swine also; and all this with so much charity, simplicity, and humility, that the man's heart was changed within him, and he threw himself at Brothers Juniper's feet, acknowledging with many tears the injuries which by word and deed he had done to him and his brethren.

Then he went and killed the swine, and having cut it up, he brought it, with many tears and great devotion, to St. Mary of the Angels, and gave it to those holy friars in compensation for the injury he had done them. Then St. Francis, considering the simplicity and patience under adversity of this good Brother Juniper, said to his companions and those who stood by: "Would to God, my brethren, that I had a forest of such Junipers!"

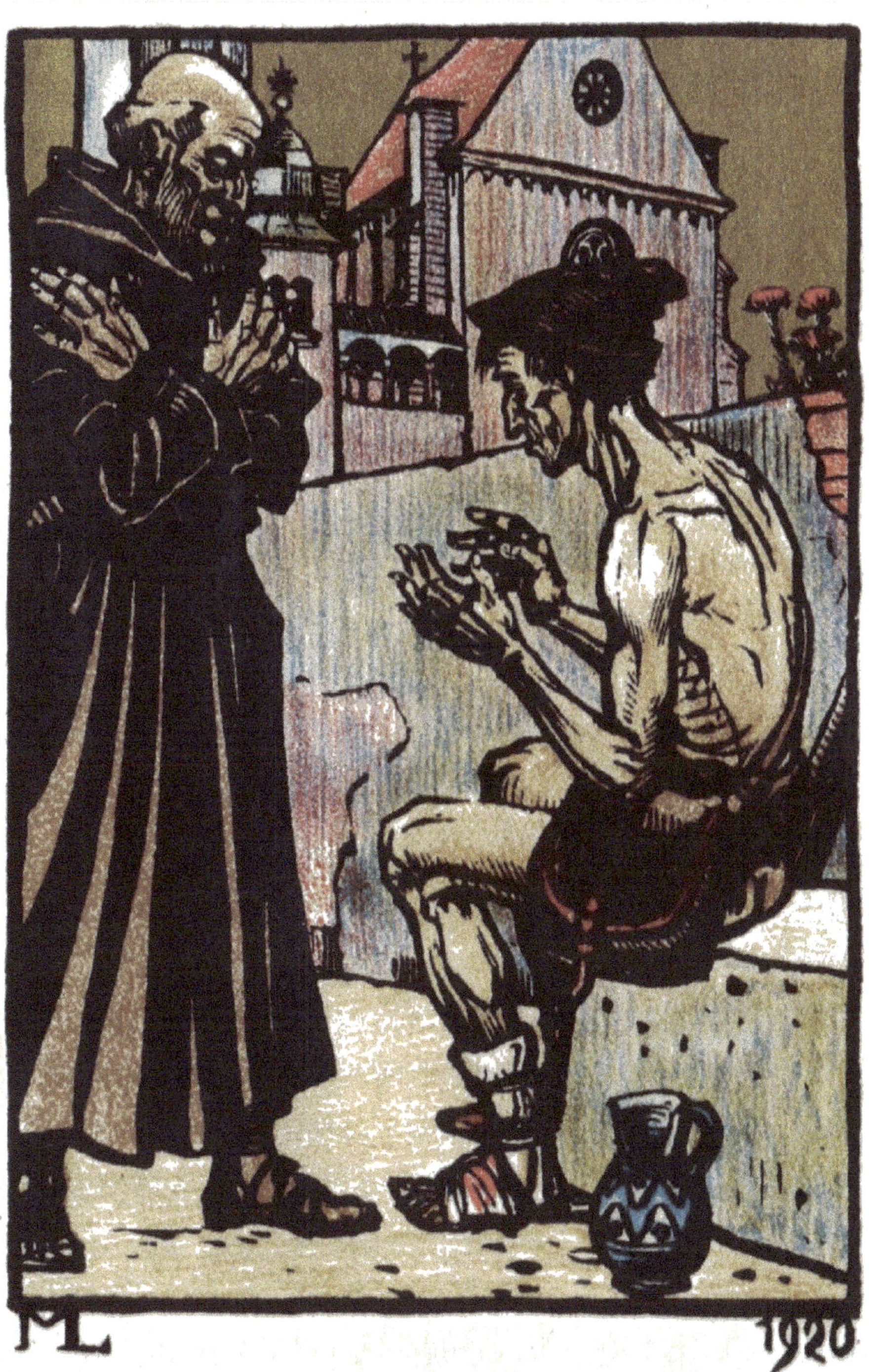

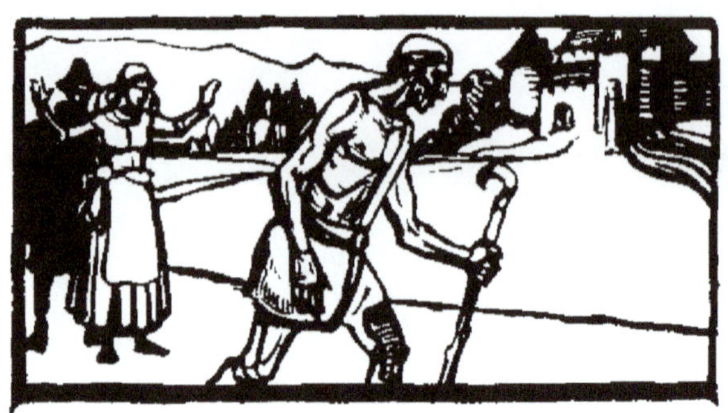

ONCE when Brother Juniper was dwelling in the valley of Spoleto, knowing that there was to be a great solemnity at Assisi, and that many were resorting thither with great devotion, it came into his head to go there also; and you shall hear in what guise he went.

He stripped himself of all but his inner garment, and thus, passing through the midst of the city of Spoleto, he came to the convent. The brethren, much displeased and scandalised, rebuked him sharply, calling him a fool, a madman, and a disgrace to the Order of St. Francis, and declaring that he ought to be put in chains as a madman.

And the general, who was then on the spot, calling all the friars together, gave Brother Juniper a very sharp correction in the presence of them all. And, after many words, he ended with this severe sentence: "So great and grievous is thy fault, that I know not what sufficient penance to give thee."

Then, Brother Juniper, answered, as one who delighted in his own confusion: "Father, I will tell you: for penance, send me back again from this solemnity in the same garb in which I came to it."

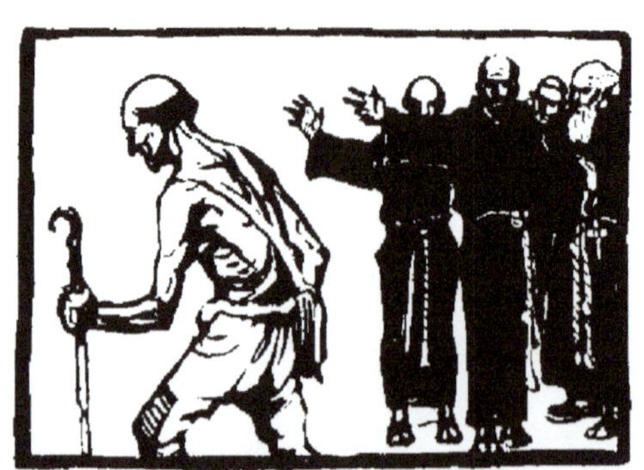

Of the
Sacred and Holy Stigmata
of Saint Francis and
Certain Considerations
Thereon

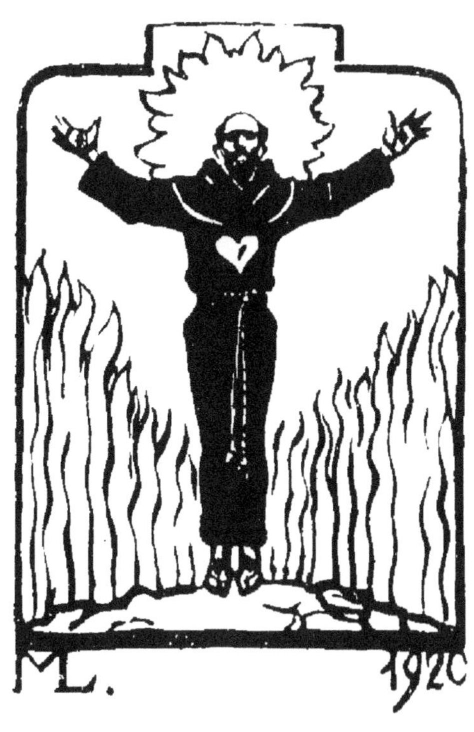

N THIS PART we will treat, with sundry devout considerations, of the glorious, sacred, and holy stigmata of our blessed father St. Francis, which he received from Christ on the holy mountain of Alvernia. And inasmuch as the said stigmata were five, according to the five wounds of our Lord Jesus Christ, therefore this treatise shall have five considerations.

The first consideration shall be of the manner in which St. Francis came to the holy mountain of Alvernia. The second consideration shall be of his life and conversation with his companions on the same holy mountain. The third consideration shall be of the seraphical apparition, and the impression of the most sacred stigmata. The fourth consideration shall be of the descent of St. Francis from Mount Alvernia after he had received the sacred stigmata, and of his return to St. Mary of the Angels. The fifth consideration shall be of certain apparitions and divine revelations vouchsafed, after the death of St. Francis, to certain holy friars and other devout persons, concerning these sacred and glorious stigmata.

OF THE FIRST CONSIDERATION OF THE SACRED, HOLY STIG-MATA

ONCERNING the first consideration, be it known that in the year 1224, being in his forty-third year, St. Francis went, by the inspiration of God, from the Valley of Spoleto into Romagna, taking with him Brother Leo as his companion; and on their way they passed by the Castle of Montefeltro, where was a great concourse of people, and a solemn banquet held, by reason that one of the Counts of Montefeltro was that day to receive his knighthood. And when St. Francis heard of this solem-

nity, and that many gentlemen of various countries were gathered together there, he said to Brother Leo, "Come, let us go up unto this festival; for, by God's help, we shall gather therefrom rich spiritual fruit."

Now, among other men of high degree who had come together to this feast, there was a certain gentleman of Tuscany who was both rich and mighty. He was called Orlando da Chiusi di Casentino; and for the marvelous things which he had heard concerning the holiness and the miracles of St. Francis he bore him great devotion, and had an exceeding desire to see him and to hear him preach.

St. Francis, then, being come to this castle, entered into the courtyard where all those gentlemen were assembled; and, in fervor of spirit, he mounted on a low wall, and began to preach, choosing for the theme of his discourse these words in the vulgar tongue: *So great is the joy which I expect, that all pain is joy to me.* And upon this theme, by the direction of the Holy Ghost, he preached so profoundly and so devoutly, proving it by the diverse pains and sufferings of the holy apostles and martyrs, and by the manifold tribulations and temptations of holy virgins and all other saints, that all that multitude of men hung upon his words both with their ears and hearts, hearkening to him as to an angel of God.

Among whom the said Orlando, being touched in the heart by God through the marvelous preaching of St. Francis, was led to speak to him after the sermon regarding the state of his soul. So taking him aside, he said to him, "O Father, I would fain take counsel with thee concerning the salvation of my soul."

St. Francis answered him, "It pleaseth me well: but go now and pay respect to thy friends, who have bidden thee to this feast, and dine with them; and after dinner we will speak together as much as it shall please thee."

Orlando, therefore, went to dine, and after dinner returning again to St. Francis, he discoursed with him at length concerning the state of his soul, and in the end he said to him, "I have a mountain in Tuscany, a devout and solitary place, called Mount Alvernia, far from all discourse of men, well fitted for one who would do penance for his sins, or who desires to lead a solitary life; if it please thee, I will freely give it to thee and thy companions for the welfare of my soul."

When St. Francis heard of this bountiful offer of a thing which he had greatly desired, he was exceeding glad, and thanking and praising God in the first place, and after him Orlando, he thus replied: "Orlando, as soon as thou shalt have returned to thy home, I will send to thee some of our brethren, to whom thou shalt show this place; and if it shall seem to them well fitted for prayer and penance, I will at once accept thy charitable offer." Having said thus, St. Francis departed, returning to St. Mary of the Angels; and Orlando likewise returned to his castle, which was called Chiusi, and was about a mile distant from Mount Alvernia.

St. Francis then sent two of his companions to the said Orlando, who received them with much charity and gladness; and he sent with them to Mount Alvernia fully fifty men-at-arms, to be their defense against wild beasts. And these brethren, being thus accompanied, ascended the mount, and searched diligently, until at last they came to a spot well fitted for devout contemplation; and this they chose for the habitation of St. Francis, and, with the help of the men-at-arms in their company, they made some little cells with branches of trees; and thus they accepted Mount Alvernia, taking possession of it in the name of God, and forthwith returned again unto St. Francis.

The saint rejoiced greatly at what they told him, and, thanking and praising God, spoke with a joyful countenance to these friars, saying, "My children, we draw near to our Lent of St. Michael the Archangel. I firmly believe it to be the will of God that we keep this Lent upon Mount Alvernia, which, by divine dispensation, has been prepared for us, that we by penance may merit from our Lord the consolation of consecrating this blessed mount to the honor and glory of God, of His glorious Mother the Virgin Mary, and of the holy angels."

And having said this, St. Francis took with him Brother Masseo da Marignano of Assisi; and Brother Angelo Tancredi of Rieti, who, in the world, had been a noble knight, and was still noted for his gentle courtesy; and Brother Leo, who was a man of the greatest simplicity and purity, for the which cause St. Francis loved him greatly. And with these three brethren St. Francis betook himself to prayer, then, having recommended himself and his companions to the prayers of the brethren who were left behind, he set forth with these three, in the name of Jesus Christ crucified, to go to Mount Alvernia.

And on the way he called Brother Masseo to him, and said: "Thou, Brother Masseo, shalt be our guardian and our superior of this journey, both in the way and while we sojourn together on the mount; and we will observe our wonted custom, which is, that one while we will keep silence; and we will take no thought beforehand of eating, or drinking, or sleeping, but when the evening comes we will beg a little bread, and stay and rest ourselves in that place which God shall prepare for us."

Then these three comrades bowed their heads, and making the sign of the cross went on their way; and the first evening they came to a house of the brethren, and there abode. The second evening, because the weather was bad and they were weary, they could not reach any house of friars, neither any town nor castle; wherefore, when night came on, they took shelter in a ruined and deserted church, and there laid them down to rest.

Now, while his companions slept, St. Francis betook himself to prayer; and, behold, in the first watch of the night there came to him a multitude of the most fierce demons who, with great noise and frenzy, began to attack him on all sides, in order to disturb him in his prayer; but this they could not do, because God was with him. When, therefore, St. Francis had endured that conflict a long time, he began to cry aloud: "O accursed spirits, you can do nothing save by the divine permission; wherefore I bid you, on behalf of the omnipotent God, to do with my body whatsoever He shall permit you to do, and most willingly will I endure it; because I have no greater enemy than my body, and therefore if you will avenge me upon it you shall do me good service."

Then did the devils begin to torment him worse than ever. But he cried out, and said: "O my Lord Jesus Christ, I thank Thee for this Thy love when the Lord punisheth His servant well in this life, that so he may not be punished in the other. And I am ready gladly to endure every pain and suffering which Thou, my God, art pleased to send me for my sins."

Then the devils dispersed and left him, being vanquished and confounded by his penance and constancy. And St. Francis in great fervor of spirit left the church and went into the wood hard by, and there, beating his breast with sighs and tears, sought after Jesus, the beloved of his soul. And having found Him at last, in the secret of his heart, now he spoke to Him reverently as his Lord, now he made answer to Him as his judge, now he besought Him as his father, now he conversed with Him as his friend. On that night and in that wood, his companions, being awake and listening to him, heard him with many tears and cries implore the divine mercy on behalf of sinners. He was heard to weep aloud for the Passion of Christ as if he had beheld it with his bodily eyes. On that same night also he was seen praying with arms outstretched in the form of a cross, and thus was he lifted up and suspended for a long time in the air, surrounded with a dazzling glory. And so, in these holy exercises, he passed all that night without sleeping.

And the next morning, his companions, knowing that he was too weak to walk, went to a poor laboring man of the country, and prayed him, for the love of God, to lend his ass to Brother Francis their father, for he was not able to travel on foot.

When the poor man heard them speak of Brother Francis, he asked them: "Are you, then, of the brethren of that friar of Assisi of whom men speak so much good?" Then the friars made answer that it was even he for whom they would borrow the ass. Then that good man made ready the ass with great care and devotion, and brought it to St. Francis, and with great reverence caused him to mount thereon. So the brethren set forth again, the poor man following behind his ass.

Now when they had gone forward a little, the peasant said to St. Francis: "Tell me, art thou Brother Francis of Assisi?"

And St. Francis answered, "Yes."

"Take heed, then," said the peasant, "that thou be in truth as good as all men account thee; for many have great faith in thee, and therefore I admonish thee to be no other than what the people take thee for."

When St. Francis heard these words, he was not angry at being thus admonished by a peasant, neither did he say within himself, as many a proud friar who in our days wears his habit would say: "What right has such a creature as this to admonish me?" But instantly dismounting from the ass, he knelt down upon the ground before that poor man; and kissing his feet, humbly thanked him for his charitable admonition. Then the peasant, together with the companions of St. Francis, with great devotion raised him from the ground, and placed him again upon the ass, and so went on their way.

And then they were come to about the midst of the ascent of the mount, because the way was toilsome, and the heat exceeding great, the peasant was overcome with thirst, insomuch that he began to cry after St. Francis saying: "Alas! Alas! I am dying of thirst; unless I have something to drink, I shall presently faint."

Then St. Francis dismounted from the ass, and betook himself to prayer, remaining upon his knees, with hands uplifted up to heaven, until he knew by revelation that his prayer was heard. Then said he to the peasant: "Run quickly to yonder rock, and there thou shalt find a stream of living water, which Jesus Christ of His mercy has caused to flow out from the stone."

Then went he to the place which St. Francis had shown to him, and found a beautiful fountain, issuing by virtue of the prayer of St. Francis, from that hard rock; and he drank of it plentifully, and was refreshed. And certain it is that this spring of water flowed forth miraculously at the prayer of St. Francis, for neither before nor after was a spring to be found at that spot, nor any running water save at a great distance therefrom. This done, St. Francis, with his companions and the peasant, returned thanks to God for the miracle thus vouchsafed, and went on their way.

And when they drew near to the rock of Alvernia, it pleased St. Francis to rest awhile under an oak, which grew by the way, and is still to be seen there, and from thence he began to consider the position of the place and the country. And while he was thus considering, behold there came a great multitude of birds from diverse regions, which, by singing and clapping their wings, testified to their great joy and gladness, and surrounded St. Francis in such wise that some perched upon his shoulders, some on his arms, some on his bosom, and others at his feet, which when his companions and the peasant saw, they marveled greatly; but St. Francis, being joyful at heart, said to them: "I believe, dearest brethren, that our Lord Jesus Christ is pleased that we should dwell on this solitary mount, inasmuch as our little brothers and sisters, the birds, show such joy at our coming."

And having said these words, he arose and proceeded to the place which had been fixed upon by his companions; and so did St. Francis come to the holy mount of Alvernia.

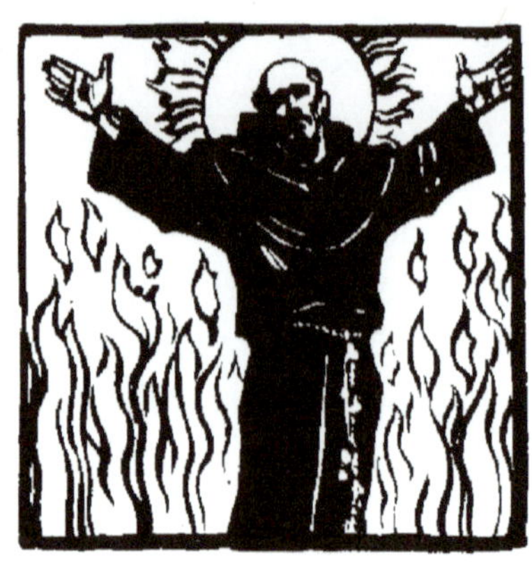

OF THE SECOND CONSIDERATION OF THE SACRED, HOLY STIGMATA

HE SECOND consideration is of the conversation of St. Francis and his companions upon Mount Alvernia. Be it known, then, that when Orlando heard that St. Francis with three companions was come to dwell on Mount Alvernia, he was filled with exceeding joy, and on the morrow he came with many others from his castle to visit St. Francis, bringing with him bread and wine, and other things necessary for him and his companions; and when he came thither, he found them in prayer, and drawing near he saluted them.

Then St. Francis arose, and with great joy and charity received Orlando and his company; and so they began to converse together. And after they had spoken together for some time, and St. Francis had thanked him for the devout solitude which he had bestowed upon them and for his coming to visit them there, he prayed Orlando to cause a little cell to be made for him at the foot of a beautiful beech tree, which was about a stone's throw from the place where they now were; and this Orlando immediately caused to be done.

Then, because evening was drawing on, and it was now time for them to depart, St. Francis preached to them for a little space; and when he had finished preaching, and had given them his blessing, Orlando called St. Francis and his companions aside, and said to them: "My dearest brothers, never was it my intention that you should be exposed on this savage mountain to any corporal necessity, which might hinder you from attending perfectly to things spiritual; wherefore it is my desire—and I say it to you now once for all—that you send freely to my house for everything you want, and if you fail to do so, I shall take it very ill at your hands." And so saying, he departed with his company and returned to his castle.

Then St. Francis caused his companions to sit down, and taught them the manner of life they were to keep, that they might live religiously in their solitude; and among other things, most earnestly did he enjoin on them the strict observance of holy poverty, saying: "Let not Orlando's charitable offer cause you in any way to offend against our lady and mistress, Holy Poverty. Hold it for certain that, the more we keep aloof from her, the more will the world keep aloof from us, and the greater want shall we endure: but if we closely embrace Holy Poverty, the world will come after us, and will minister to us abundantly. God has called us into holy religion for the salvation of the world, and has made this compact between the world and us—that we should give it good example, and that it should provide for our necessities. Let us, then, persevere in holy poverty; for it is the way to perfection, and the pledge of eternal riches."

And after many devout and holy words, he thus concluded: "This is the manner of life which I impose upon you and upon myself; and because I behold my death approaching, I purpose to remain in solitude to recollect myself in God, and to weep over my sins in His sight. Therefore, when it shall so please him, let Brother Leo bring me a little bread and water, and on no account suffer any secular to come near me; but do you answer for me to them." And having thus said, he gave them his blessing, and went his way to his cell under the beech tree; and his companions remained behind, full purposed to obey his commands.

Now a few days afterwards, as St. Francis was considering the formation of the mountain, and marveling at the great fissures and openings in the solid rock, it was revealed to him by God in prayer that these strange caverns had been made miraculously at the hour of the Passion of Christ, when, according to the Evangelist's words, the rocks were rent; and this was by the will of God, who manifested himself thus wonderfully upon Mount Alvernia, because there the Passion of our Lord Jesus Christ was to be renewed in the soul of His servant by love and compassion, and in his body by the impression of the sacred, holy stigmata.

When St. Francis had received this revelation, he forthwith shut himself up in his cell, and, in great recollection of soul, prepared himself for the mystery which was to be revealed to him; and from that time forth, he began to taste more frequently the sweetness of divine contemplation, by which he was sometimes so absorbed in God, that he was seen by his companions to be raised corporally above the ground, and rapt in prayer; and in these raptures were revealed to St. Francis not only things present and future, but even the secret thoughts and desires of the brethren, as was experienced by Brother Leo, his companion in those days.

For this same Brother Leo, being beset by a most grievous spiritual temptation, felt a great longing to have some devout thing written by the hand of St. Francis, feeling assured that, if he had it, the temptation would leave him, either wholly or in part. But, either out of shame or reverence, he dared not speak of his desire to St. Francis, to whom nevertheless it was revealed by the Holy Ghost; whereupon he called the brother to him, and bade him bring him wherewithal to write, and with his own hand he wrote a verse in honor of Christ, drawing at the foot thereof the sign of a cross *Tau:* and according to Brother Leo's desire, he gave it to him, saying, "Take this writing, dearest brother, and keep it most diligently till the day of thy death. May God bless thee, and guard thee from all temptation! But if temptation come unto thee, be not afraid, for I hold thee to be more truly the servant of God, and more worthy of love the harder thou art oppressed by temptation. And I tell thee in all sincerity, that no man should account himself to be a perfect friend of God until he has passed through manifold temptations and tribulations."

Now when Brother Leo had received this writing with great faith and devotion, at once all the temptation departed from him; and returning to his companions, he told them with great joy of the grace which he had received from God through that writing of St. Francis; and the brethren laid it up and kept it diligently, and by it they were enabled to work many miracles.

And from that day forward, Brother Leo set himself with a good and pure intention to scrutinize and attentively consider the life of St. Francis; and in reward of his purity he was permitted many times to behold him rapt in God and suspended above the earth, sometimes at the height of three feet above the ground, sometimes four, sometimes raised as high as the top of the beech trees, and sometimes exalted so high in the air, and surrounded with so dazzling a glory, that he could scarce endure to look upon him. And what did this simple friar do when St. Francis, in his raptures, was thus raised above his reach? He would go softly behind him and, with tears, embrace and kiss his feet, saying: "My God, have mercy upon me, a sinner, and by the merits of this holy man let me find grace in Thy sight."

And once when he was standing beneath the feet of St. Francis, who was raised so high that he could not touch him, he saw a scroll descend from heaven and rest upon his head, whereon were these words, written in letters of gold: *Here abideth the grace of God!* And when he had read the scroll, he saw it return again to heaven.

By the gift of the grace of God which dwelt in him, St. Francis was not only absorbed in God by ecstatic contemplation, but was comforted often by angelical visitations. One day when he was meditating upon his death, and upon what might hereafter befall his Order, he said: "O Lord God, when I am dead, what will become of this Thy poor family, which in Thy goodness Thou hast committed to me, a sinner? Who will comfort, who will correct, who will pray to Thee for it?" Then did an angel of God appear to him, and comfort him with these words: "I declare to thee, on behalf of God, that thine Order shall never fail until the day of judgment; and no sinner, be he ever so great, who bears a hearty love to this thine Order shall not find mercy with God; nor shall any man live long who maliciously persecutes it. Nor shall any evil-doer who refuses to amend his life long persevere in thine Order. And be not thou troubled if thou perceive some brethren who are not good, and observe not the rule as they ought to do, and fear not lest on that account this Order of religion will fail; for there shall always be many and many a one who will observe with great perfection the life of Christ's Gospel, and the purity of the rule; and all these, after their bodily life is ended, shall enter into life eternal, without passing through purgatory. Others will observe it, but not per-fectly; and these, before they reach paradise, shall remain for a while in purgatory; but the time of their purification God will commit unto thee. But of those who in no way observe the rule, take thou no care, saith the Lord; for neither doth He care for them." And when the angel had said these words, he departed, leaving St. Francis greatly strengthened and consoled.

And now the Feast of our Lady's Assumption drew near, and St. Francis sought for a more secret and solitary place in which he might spend alone the Lent of St. Michael the Archangel, which begins on the Feast of the Assumption.

Wherefore he called Brother Leo, and said thus to him: "Go and stand at the door of the brethren's oratory, and when I shall call thee, turn to me." And Brother Leo went and stood at the door, and St. Francis went away a space, and called aloud, and Brother Leo heard and turned towards him. Then St. Francis said: "My sons, let us seek for some more secret place, where thou wilt not hear me when I call thus to thee."

And when they had searched the mount, they found a place on the northern side most secret and well fitted for the purpose, but they could not reach it because of a frightful chasm in the rock; across this chasm they cast a tree to serve for a bridge, and so passed over.

Then St. Francis sent for the other friars, and told them that he purposed to spend the Lent of St. Michael in that solitary place, and prayed them, therefore, to make for him a little cell, so that, though he could cry aloud, he might not be heard by them. And when the cell was made, he said to them: "Return now to your place and leave me here, without any disturbance or perturbation of mind; therefore let none of you come unto me, nor suffer any secular person to come near the cell. But thou only, Brother Leo, once a day shalt come to me with a little bread and water, and once a night at the hour of Matins, and thou shalt come in silence; and when thou art upon the bridge thou shalt say, *Domine, labia mea aperies;* and if I answer thee, thou shalt come to the cell, and we will say Matins together; and if I do not answer thee, thou shalt depart forthwith." And this St. Francs said, because he was sometimes so absorbed in God that he heard nothing, nor felt anything by his bodily senses. And having thus spoken, he gave them his blessing, and they returned to their place.

Thus, on the Feast of the Assumption, St. Francis began the holy Lent, with great abstinence and austerity, macerating his body and invigorating his soul by fervent prayers, vigils, and disciplines; and thus increasing more and more, and going from virtue to virtue, he prepared his soul to receive divine mysteries and illuminations, and his body to sustain the cruel conflicts with the demons who often attacked him sensibly.

And it befell one day in this Lent that St. Francis, going forth from his cell in great fervor of spirit, went to pray in a cave hollowed out of a rock at the top of a steep and frightful precipice, when the devil suddenly appeared before him in a terrible form, and sought to hurl him to the bottom. St. Francis, being unable to fly or to endure the horrible aspect of the devil, turned his face, hands, and whole body towards the rock, and recommended himself to God, groping with his hands, yet finding nothing to which he might cling. But, as it pleased God, who never suffers His servants to be tempted beyond what they are able to bear, the rock suddenly opened and received his body within it; and, as if he had placed his hands and face in liquid wax, the form of the hands and face of St. Francis remained impressed upon the stone; and thus, by the help of God, he escaped out of the hands of the devil.

But the injury which the devil could not then do to St. Francis by casting him down the precipice, he inflicted long after his death upon one of his beloved and devoted brethren, who was standing in the same spot preparing some planks of wood for the safe passage of those who should come to the place out of devotion to St. Francis and the miracle which had been wrought there.

For one day, when he had a heavy piece of wood on his shoulder, the devil cast him down thus laden to the bottom of the rock. But God, who had preserved St. Francis from falling, by his merits delivered the devout friar from all injury in his fall; for as he fell, with a loud voice and great devotion he recommended himself to St. Francis, who immediately appeared to him, and taking him in his arms, set him down at the bottom of the rock without suffering any injury whatsoever.

The brethren, who had heard his cry when he fell, believing that he was assuredly dead, and that he had been dashed to pieces by his fall from so great a height upon those pointed rocks, taking a bier went round the mountain by another way, with great weeping and lamentation, to collect his mangled remains and give them burial. Having, then, descended the mountain, behold, the brother who had fallen met them with the wood on his shoulder with which he fell, singing the *Te Deum* with a loud voice. And the brethren marveling greatly thereat, he related to them in order the manner of his fall, and how St. Francis had delivered him from all danger. Then all the brethren came with him to the place, devoutly chanting the *Te Deum,* and praising and thanking God and St. Francis for the miracle that had been wrought in their brother.

St. Francis, then, passing this Lent, as has been said, in the midst of these conflicts with the devil, received many consolations from God, not only by angelic visitations, but through the ministry of the wild mountain birds. For, through all that Lent, a falcon, whose nest was hard by his cell, awakened him every night a little before the hour of Matins by her cry and the flapping of her wings, and would not leave him till he had risen to say Matins; and if at any time St. Francis was more sick than usual, or weak, or weary, this falcon, like a discreet and charitable Christian, would call him somewhat later than was her wont. Now St. Francis took great delight in this clock of his, because the great carefulness of the falcon drove away all sloth and summoned him to prayer; and, moreover, during the daytime, she would often abide familiarly with him.

To conclude this second consideration, St. Francis, being much weakened in body both by his great abstinence and by his conflicts with the devil, and desiring to strengthen his body by the spiritual food of the soul, began to meditate upon the unbounded joy and glory of the blessed heaven; and he besought of God to grant him some little foretaste of its bliss. Now while this thought was in his mind, suddenly an angel appeared to him in surpassing glory, having a viol in his left hand and a bow in his right. And as St. Francis stood in amazement at the sight, the angel drew the bow once across the strings of the viol, when the soul of St. Francis was instantly so ravished by the sweetness of the melody, that all his bodily senses were suspended, and he believed, as he afterwards told his companions, that, if the sound had been continued, the intolerable sweetness would have drawn his soul from his body. And so much for the second consideration.

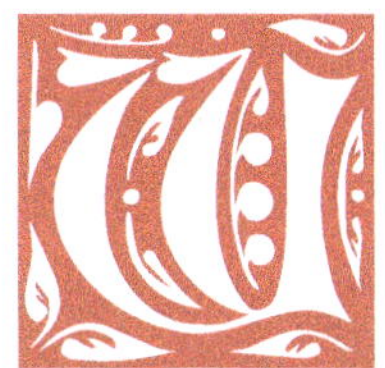E ARE COME NOW to the third consideration, namely, of the seraphical apparition, and the impression of the sacred, holy stigmata. As the Feast of the Holy Cross then drew nigh, in the month of September, Brother Leo went one night at his accustomed hour to say Matins with St. Francis. When he came to the bridge, he said, as he was wont to do, *Domine, labia mea aperies;* but St. Francis made no answer.

Yet Brother Leo turned not back as he had been commanded to do, but with a good and holy intention, he passed the bridge and went straight into the cell; but there he found not St. Francis. Thinking, therefore, that he was gone to pray in some solitary place, he went softly through the wood, seeking him in the moonlight.

At last he heard his voice, and drawing near, beheld him kneeling in prayer with his face and hands lifted up towards heaven, and crying, in fervor of spirit: "Who art Thou, my dearest Lord? And who am I, a most vile worm and Thy most unprofitable servant?"—and these words he repeated over and over again, adding nothing more.

At this Brother Leo, greatly marveling, lifted up his eyes to heaven and beheld a torch of most intense and glorious fire, which seemed to descend and alight upon the head of St. Francis; and from the flame there seemed to issue forth a voice which spake with him, but Brother Leo knew not the words which were spoken.

Hearing this, and accounting himself unworthy to stand in that holy place, and fearing also to offend St. Francis and to disturb him by his presence, he went away silently, and stood afar off to behold what would follow; and looking earnestly upon St. Francis, he saw him thrice spread forth his hands to the flame, and after a long time he beheld it mount again to heaven. Then he turned joyfully to go back to his cell, being greatly consoled by the visitation.

But, as he turned, St. Francis heard the rustling of the leaves under his feet, and commanded him not to stir, but to await his coming. And Brother Leo in obedience stood still, and waited in such great fear that, as he afterwards told his companions, he would have wished that the earth might swallow him up rather than wait for St. Francis, whose anger he feared exceedingly; for he took great heed always not to offend him, lest he should be deprived of his company.

When St. Francis, then, came up to him, he said: "Who art thou?," and Brother Leo, in fear and trembling, answered: "Father, I am Brother Leo."

And St. Francis said to him: "Wherefore hast thou come hither, dear brother? Did I not forbid thee to observe me? Tell me now, by holy obedience, whether thou hast seen or heard anything?"

And Brother Leo replied: "Father, I heard thee speak and say many times, 'Who art Thou, my dearest Lord, and who am I, a most vile worm and Thy most unprofitable servant?'" And then, kneeling before St. Francis, Brother Leo accused himself of disobedience to his command, and besought him to expound to him the meaning of the words which he had heard, and to tell him also those which he had not heard.

Then St. Francis, seeing that, for his simplicity and purity, God had revealed so much to Brother Leo, condescended to reveal and expound also that which he desired further to know; and thus he spoke to him: "Know, dearest brother, that when I said those words which thou didst hear, two great lights were before my soul, the one the knowledge of myself, the other the knowledge of the Creator.

"When I said: 'Who art Thou, my dearest Lord?,' I was in a light of contemplation, in which I beheld the abyss of the infinite goodness and wisdom and power of God; and when I said: 'Who am I?,' I was in a light of contemplation wherein I saw the lamentable abyss of my own vileness and misery; wherefore I said: 'Who art Thou, the Lord of infinite wisdom and goodness, who dost vouchsafe to visit me, a vile worm and abominable?' And in that flame which thou didst behold was God, who under that appearance spake to me, as of old He spake to Moses.

"And among other things which He said to me, He asked of me three gifts; and I made answer: 'O Lord, I am nothing; Thou knowest full well that I have nothing else but my cord and my tunic, and even these are Thine; what, then, can I offer or give to Thy Majesty?'

"Then He said to me: 'Search in thy bosom, and offer me what thou shalt find there.' And searching, I found there a golden ball, and I offered it to God; and the like I did three times, even as God commanded me;

and then I knelt down thrice, and blessed and gave thanks to God, who had thus given me something to offer Him.

"And immediately it was given to me to understand that these three offerings signified most holy obedience, most entire poverty, and most pure chastity, which God by His grace has enabled me so perfectly to observe that I have nothing to reproach myself thereupon. And whereas thou didst see me put my hand into my bosom and offer to God those three virtues, signified by these three golden balls which God had placed in my bosom, so God has infused such virtue into my soul, that for all the gifts and graces which of His sovereign bounty He has bestowed upon me, I should always with heart and voice praise and magnify Him.

"These are the words which thou didst hear when thou didst see me thrice lift up my hands. But take heed, brother little lamb, that thou observe me no more, but return to thy cell with the blessing of God; and take heed to my words, for yet a few days, and God will work such strange and marvelous things upon this mountain as shall astonish the whole world; for He will do a new thing which He hath never done before to any creature upon this earth."

And when he had said these words, he bade him bring the book of the Gospels, because God had put it into his mind that, by thrice opening that book, he should learn what God would be pleased to do with him. And when the book was brought to him, St. Francis went to prayer; and when he had prayed, he caused Brother Leo to open the book three times in the name of the Most Holy Trinity; and, by the divine disposal, it opened each time at the Passion of Christ. And by this it was given him to understand that, even as he had followed Christ in the actions of his life, so should he follow and be confirmed to Him in the sufferings and afflictions of His Passion, before he should pass out of this life.

And from that day forward St. Francis began to taste more abundantly the sweetness of divine contemplation, and of divine visitations, among which he had one, preparatory to the impression of the sacred, holy stigmata, after the following manner.

The day before the Feast of the Most Holy Cross, as St. Francis was praying secretly in his cell, an angel of God appeared to him, and spake to him thus from God: "I am come to admonish and encourage thee, that thou prepare thyself to receive in all patience and humility that which God will give and do to thee."

St. Francis replied: "I am ready to bear patiently whatsoever my Lord shall be pleased to do to me"; and so the angel departed.

On the following day—being the Feast of the Holy Cross—St. Francis was praying before daybreak at the entrance of his cell, and turning his face towards the east, he prayed in these words: "O Lord Jesus Christ, two graces do I ask of Thee before I die; the first, that in my lifetime I may feel, as far as possible, both in my soul and body, that pain which Thou, sweet Lord, didst endure in the hour of Thy most bitter Passion; the second, that I may feel in my heart as much as possible of that excess of love by which Thou, O Son of God, wast inflamed to suffer so cruel a Passion for us sinners." And continuing a long time in that prayer, he understood that God had heard him, and that, so far as is possible for a mere creature, he should be permitted to feel these things.

Having then received this promise, St. Francis began to contemplate most devoutly the Passion of Jesus Christ and His infinite charity; and so greatly did the fervor of devotion increase within him, that he was all transformed into Jesus by love and compassion. And being thus inflamed in that contemplation, on that same morning he beheld a seraph descending from heaven with six fiery and resplendent wings; and this seraph with rapid flight drew nigh unto St. Francis, so that he could plainly discern Him, and perceive that He bore the image of one crucified; and the wings were so disposed, that two were spread over the head, two were outstretched in flight, and the other two covered the whole body.

And when St. Francis beheld it, he was much afraid, and filled at once with joy and grief and wonder. He felt great joy at the gracious presence of Christ, who appeared to him thus familiarly, and looked upon him thus lovingly, but, on the other hand, beholding Him thus crucified, he felt exceeding grief and compassion. He marveled much at so stupendous and unwonted a vision, knowing well that the infirmity of the Passion accorded ill with the immortality of the seraphic spirit. And in that perplexity of mind it was revealed to him by Him who thus appeared, that by divine providence this vision had been thus shown to him that he might understand that, not by martyrdom of the body, but by a consuming fire of the soul, he was to be transformed into the express image of Christ

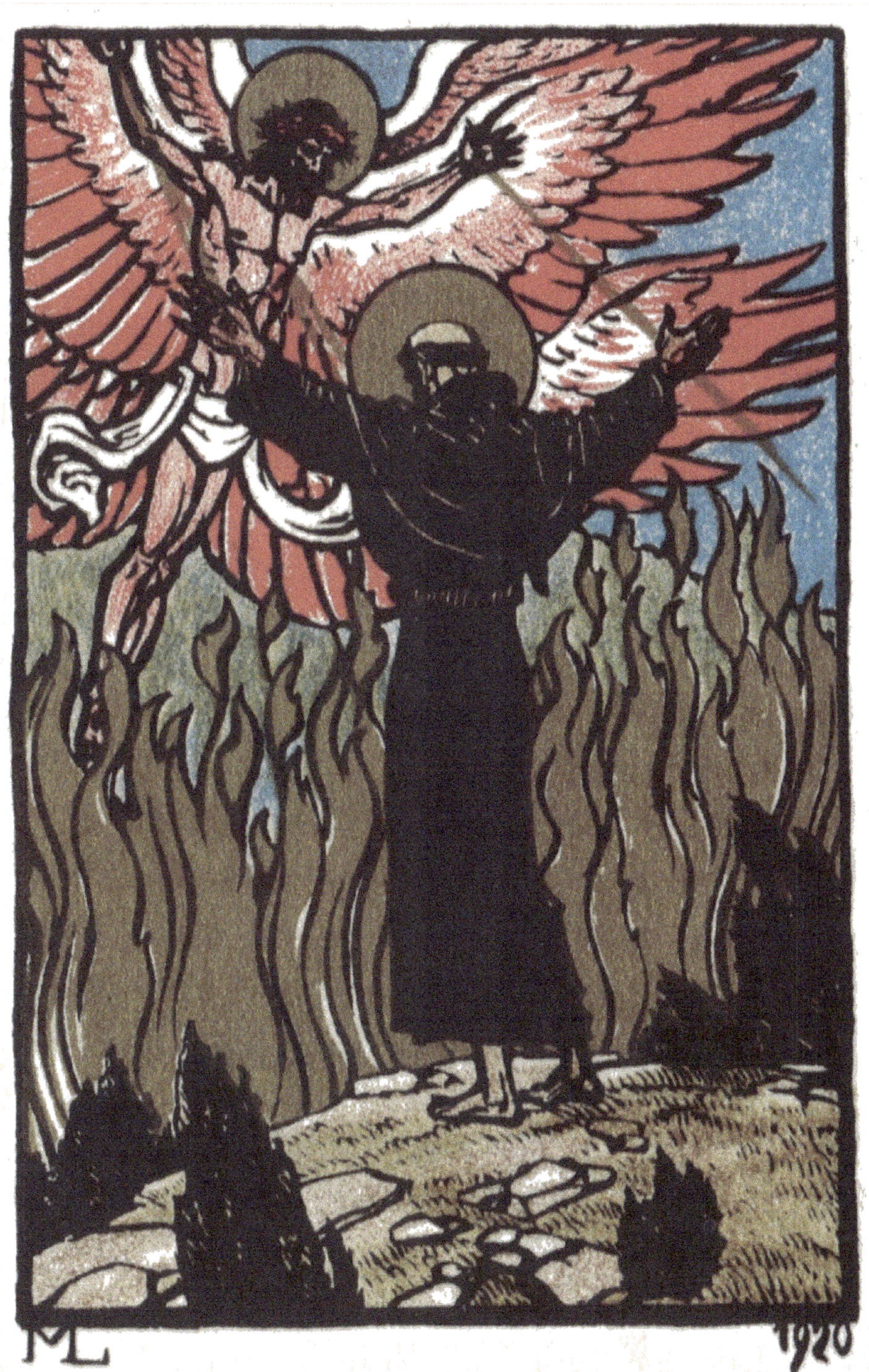

crucified in that wonderful apparition.

Then did all of Mount Alvernia appear wrapped in intense fire, which illumined all the mountains and valleys around, as it were the sun shining in his strength upon the earth, for which cause the shepherds who were watching their flocks in that country were filled with fear, as they themselves afterwards told the brethren, affirming that this light had been visible on Mount Alvernia for upwards of an hour. And because of the brightness of that light, which shone through the windows of the inn where they were tarrying, some muleteers who were travelling in Romagna arose in haste, supposing that the sun had risen, and saddled and loaded their beasts; but as they journeyed on, they saw that light disappear, and the visible sun arise.

In this seraphical apparition, Christ, who appeared under that form to St. Francis, spoke to him certain high and secret things, which in his lifetime he would never reveal to any person, but after his death he made them known to one of the brethren, and the words were these: "Knowest thou," said Christ, "what I have done to thee? I have given thee the stigmata which are the insignia of My Passion, that thou mayest be My standard-bearer; and as on the day of My death I descended into limbo, and by virtue of these My stigmata delivered thence all the souls whom I found there, so do I grant to thee that every year on the anniversary of thy death thou mayst go to purgatory, and take with thee to the glory of paradise all the souls of thy three Orders, the Friars Minor, the Sisters, and the Penitents, and likewise all others whom thou shalt find there, who have been especially devout to thee; that so thou mayst be conformed to Me in death, as thou hast been like to Me in life."

Then, after long and secret conference together, that marvelous vision disappeared, leaving in the heart of St. Francis an excessive fire and ardor of divine love, and on his flesh a wonderful trace and image of the Passion of Christ. For upon his hands and feet began immediately to appear the figures of the nails, as he had seen them on the Body of Christ crucified, who had appeared to him in the likeness of a seraph. And thus the hands and feet appeared pierced through the midst by the nails, the heads whereof were seen outside the flesh in the palms of the hands and the soles of the feet, and the points of the nails stood out at the back of the hands and the feet in such wise that they appeared to be twisted and bent back upon themselves, and the portion thereof that was bent back or twisted stood out free from the flesh, so that one could put a finger through the same as through a ring; and the heads of the nails were round and black. In like manner, on the right side appeared the image of an unhealed wound, as if made by a lance, and still red and bleeding, from which drops of blood often flowed from the holy breast of St. Francis, staining his tunic and his drawers.

And because of this his companions, before they knew the truth from himself, perceiving that he would not uncover his hands and his feet, and that he could not set the soles of his feet upon the ground, and finding traces of blood upon his tunic when they washed it, understood of a certainty that he bore in his hands and feet and side the image and similitude of our Lord Jesus Christ crucified.

And although he labored hard to conceal these sacred stigmata holy and glorious, thus clearly impressed upon his flesh, yet finding that he could with difficulty hide them from his familiar companions, and fearing at the same time to reveal the secrets of God, he was in great doubt and trouble of mind whether or not he should make known the seraphical vision and the impression of the sacred, holy stigmata. At last, being pricked in conscience, he called together certain of the brethren, in whom he placed the greatest confidence, and proposing to them his doubt in general terms, asked their counsel on the matter.

Now among these friars there was one of great sanctity, called Brother Illuminato; and he, being truly illuminated by God, understood that St. Francis must have seen something miraculous, and said thus to him: "Know, Brother Francis, that not for thyself alone, but for others, doth God reveal to thee His secrets, and therefore thou hast cause for fear lest thou be worthy of censure if thou conceal that which, for the good of others, has been made known to thee."

Then St. Francis, being moved by these words, with great fear and reverence told them the manner of the aforesaid vision, adding that Christ, who had thus appeared to him, had said to him certain things which he might never make known so long as he should live.

Now although these sacred wounds, which had been impressed upon him by Christ, gave great joy to his heart, yet they caused unspeakable pain to his body; so that, being constrained by necessity, he made choice of Brother Leo, for his great purity and simplicity, to whom he revealed the whole matter, suffering him to touch and dress his wounds on all days except during the time from Thursday evening till Saturday morning, for then he would not by any human remedy mitigate the pain of Christ's Passion, which he bore in his body, because at that time our Savior Jesus Christ was taken and crucified, died and was buried for us. And it came to pass sometimes that when Brother Leo was removing the bandage from the wound in the side, St. Francis, because of the pain caused thereby, would lay his hand on Brother Leo's breast, and at the touch of that holy hand Brother Leo felt such sweetness of devotion as well-nigh made him to fall fainting to the ground.

To conclude, so far as concerns this third consideration, St. Francis, having completed the Lent of St. Michael the Archangel, prepared himself by divine revelation to return with Brother Leo to St. Mary of the Angels; and calling to him Brother Masseo and Brother Angelo, he commended that holy mount unto their care, and blessing them in the name of Jesus crucified, he suffered them, at their earnest prayer, to see, touch, and kiss his sacred hands adorned with those holy, glorious, and sacred stigmata; and so leaving them in great joy and consolation, he parted from them and came down from the holy mountain.

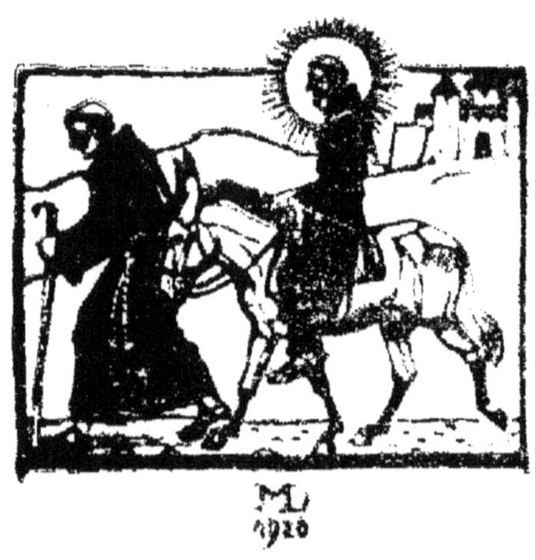

S TO THE FOURTH consideration, be it known, that after the true love of Christ had perfectly transformed St. Francis into God, and into the true image of Christ crucified, that angelical man, having fulfilled the Lent of forty days in honor of St. Michael the Archangel on the holy mountain of Alvernia, came down from the mount with Brother Leo and a devout peasant, on whose ass he rode, because, by reason of the nails in his feet, he could hardly go on foot.

And the fame of his sanctity being already spread abroad through the country by the shepherds who had seen Mount Alvernia on fire, and who took it to be a token of some great miracle wrought by God on his person, no sooner had he descended from the mountain than all the people of the country through which he passed, men and women, great and small, pressed round him, eagerly desiring to touch and kiss his hands; and though he could not altogether repress their devotion, yet, in order to conceal the sacred, holy stigmata, he wrapped bandages round his hands, and covered them with his sleeves, giving them only the fingers to kiss.

But though he thus strove to conceal the secret of the sacred stigmata, in order to shun all occasion of worldly glory, it pleased God for His own glory to work many miracles by virtue of the same holy stigmata, and especially in this journey from Mount Alvernia to St. Mary of the Angels. And the same hath He since renewed in many and diverse parts of the world, both during the lifetime of St. Francis and after his glorious death, that their mysterious and marvelous virtue, and the exceeding charity and mercy of Christ towards him, might be made manifest to the world by clear and evident miracles, such as these which follow.

At St. Francis drew near to a city on the confines of Arezzo, a woman came to him weeping bitterly, and carrying in her arms her son, a boy of eight years old, so greatly swollen with dropsy that he could not stand upright upon his feet; and laying him down before St. Francis she besought him to pray to God for him. St. Francis first betook himself to prayer, and then laying his holy hands upon the child, the swelling subsided at once, and he restored him completely cured to his mother, who received him with great joy, and took him home, thanking God and St. Francis, and taking delight in showing her restored child to all her neighbors who came to her house to witness the cure.

On the same day, St. Francis passed on through Borgo San Sepolcro; and as soon as he approached the castle, a multitude of people poured forth from the castle and the neighboring villages to meet him, many of them bearing olive-branches in their hands, and crying aloud: "Behold the saint; behold the saint!" And in their devotion and eager desire to touch him, the people pressed mightily upon him; but he, being rapt in contemplation, and his mind wholly fixed on God, although thus pressed upon and dragged hither and thither by the multitude, was insensible of all that passed around, and knew nothing of all that was said or done, or even that he had passed by that castle or through the country.

When, therefore, the multitude had returned to their own houses, and he had reached a house of lepers about a mile on the other side of the town, coming to himself as if just returned from the other world, the heavenly contemplative asked his companions: "When shall we come to the town?" For his soul, fixed and rapt in the contemplation of heaven, had been unconscious of all things earthly, and perceived neither lapse of time, nor change of place, nor persons passing by. And the like befell him many different times, as his companions often experienced.

That evening St. Francis arrived at the house of the brethren of Monte Casale, where was a friar so grievously ill, and so cruelly afflicted by his sickness, that it seemed to be rather an infliction and torment of the devil than any natural infirmity; for sometimes he would cast himself down on the ground, trembling fearfully, and foaming at the mouth. At other times every nerve in his body seemed to be distended, or contracted, or distorted, and he would spring convulsively from the ground, and immediately fall prostrate again. St. Francis, then, being seated at table, and hearing from the brethren the miserable condition of this friar, which seemed past remedy, took compassion on him, and taking a morsel of the bread which he was eating, he made the sign of the cross upon it with those holy hands that bore the stigmata of Christ, and sent it to the sick brother, who had no sooner eaten it than he was perfectly cured, and never more felt any return of his infirmity.

On the following morning St. Francis sent two of the brethren from that place to abide at Alvernia, and with them the peasant who had lent him the ass, desiring him to return to his house. And having remained a few days in that place, St. Francis departed and went to the city of Castello. And behold many of the citizens came to meet him, bringing with them a woman who for a long time past had been possessed by a devil; and they humbly besought him to deliver her, because she troubled all the country round by howling fearfully, or shrieking piteously, or at times by barking like a dog. Then St. Francis, having first prayed and made the sign of the most holy cross over her, commanded the devil to depart out of her; and forthwith he departed, leaving her whole both in mind and body.

And as the news of the miracle spread among the people, another woman full of faith brought a child sick of a grievous ulcer, and devoutly besought him to bless it with his hand. Then St. Francis, accepting her devotion, took the child, and removing the bandage, made the sign of the most holy cross thrice over the wound; and then, having bound it up again with his own hands, he delivered the child to his mother, who, as it was evening, laid him down immediately on his bed to sleep. In the morning, when she went to take him out of his bed, she found the wound unbandaged and perfectly healed, no trace remaining of it, save that in the place where it had been there was impressed the likeness of a red rose in testimony of the miracle, which remained until his death, and many a time excited him to devotion to St. Francis, by whom he had been healed.

In that city, at the desire of the devout inhabitants, St. Francis abode a month, during which time he wrought many miracles, and then departed thence to go to St. Mary of the Angels with Brother Leo and a good man who had lent him an ass on which he rode.

It so happened that, as they travelled night and day, finding no place where they could lodge for the night, they took shelter from the cold and the snow, which was falling fast, in the cavity of a hollow rock. And night coming upon them as they remained under this miserable shelter, which scarcely protected them from the inclemency of the weather, the poor man to whom the ass belonged, being unable to sleep for the cold, and having no means of kindling a fire, began to complain bitterly, and to weep and almost to murmur at St. Francis for having brought him into such a place. Then St. Francis, hearing him, had compassion on him, and in fervor of spirit stretched out his hand and touched him, when—wonderful to say—no sooner did the poor man feel the touch of that hand which had been pierced and enkindled by the seraph's fire than all sensation of cold departed from him, and such glowing heat inflamed him within and without, as if he had been placed near the mouth of a fiery furnace, that, being instantly relieved and comforted both in body and soul, he fell asleep, and slept (as he said himself) all night through till morning, more sweetly amid the rocks and snow than he had ever slept in his own bed.

Now when they had journeyed for another day, they came to St. Mary of the Angels, and as they drew nigh to it, Brother Leo lifted up his eyes and beheld a most beautiful cross, and upon it the image of the Crucified, going before St. Francis, who followed after it; so that when he stood still, the cross stood still, and when he went forward, the cross went ever before him; and such was the splendor of that cross, that it not only illumined the face of St. Francis, but made all the way bright around him, and so continued shining till he entered the convent of St. Mary of the Angels.

St. Francis, then, coming with Brother Leo, was received by the brethren with great charity and joy, and from that day forward St. Francis dwelt for the most of his time at St. Mary of the Angels until the day of his death. And as the fame of his sanctity and of his miracles went forth, more and more out of the depth of his humility did he conceal the gifts and graces of God as far as he could, calling himself the greatest of sinners.

On occasion of this Brother Leo marveling, on a certain day, considered foolishly within himself: "See now, how he calleth himself the greatest of sinners, and that before all men, when he has become great in the Order and is so much honored of God; while yet in secret he never confessed himself to be guilty of carnal sin; is it then true that he is still a virgin?"

And thenceforth there took hold of him a great longing to know the truth in this matter, yet did he not dare to ask St. Francis. Wherefore he turned himself to God, praying earnestly that He would reveal to him the truth he so much wished to know; and by his many prayers and through the merit of St. Francis he was heard, and it was answered to him that St. Francis was, in very truth, a virgin in his body, by means of the vision that followed.

For in his vision he beheld St. Francis standing in a high place and an honorable, whereto none other could attain to stand beside him; and it was said unto him in the spirit that this place, so lofty and so excellent, signified the most high virginal chastity of St. Francis, which was wholly reasonable in that flesh of his that was to be adorned with the sacred, holy stigmata of Christ.

St. Francis finding that, by reason of the stigmata of Christ, his bodily strength was gradually wasting away, and that he could no longer rule over the Order, hastened to assemble a general chapter; and the brethren being all met together, he humbly laid before them his incapacity, by reason of his infirmities, any longer to fill the office of general, although he might not resign the generalate, to which he had been appointed by the Pope, nor name a successor without his express sanction; but he nominated Brother Peter Cattani his vicar, affectionately and with all his heart recommending the Order to him and to the ministers provincial.

And having done this, St. Francis, being strengthened in spirit, raised his eyes and hands to heaven, saying thus: "To Thee, O Lord my God, to Thee do I commend Thy family, which till now Thou hast committed to me, and of which, by reason of my infirmities, as Thou knowest, O my sweetest Lord, I can now no longer take care. I commend it also to the ministers provincial, who shall render an account to Thee at the Day of Judgment if any brother perish by their negligence, or evil example, or over-sharp correction." And by these words, as it pleased God, all the brethren understood that he spoke of the sacred stigmata, which he called his infirmities, and none of them could refrain from weeping for devotion.

And thenceforth he left all the care and government of the Order in the hands of his vicar and of the ministers provincial; and he said: "Now that for my infirmities I have given over the care of the Order, I have nothing to do henceforth but to pray to God for this our religious Order, and to give a good example to the brethren. And I know moreover that, even were I freed from my infirmities, the greatest good which I could do to the Order would be to pray to God for it continually, that He would be pleased to defend and rule and preserve it."

Now, as we have said before, St. Francis did all in his power to conceal the sacred, holy stigmata, for after he received them he kept always his hands and feet covered; yet could he not hinder that many times several of the brethren contrived to see and touch them, and especially the wound of the side, which with the greatest diligence he sought to conceal.

Thus a brother who waited on him, having one day persuaded him to take off his tunic in his presence that he might shake the dust out of it, clearly saw the wound in the side; and thrusting his hand suddenly into the bosom of St. Francis, he touched it with three fingers, ascertaining its length and breadth: and in like manner it was discovered at another time by his vicar.

But it was attested still more clearly by Brother Ruffino, a man of most sublime contemplation, of whom St. Francis was wont to say that in all the world he knew not a holier man; so that for his great sanctity he loved him most heartily and granted to him all he desired. In three several ways did this Brother Ruffino certify both himself and others of the reality of the sacred, holy stigmata, and especially of that in the side.

The first was that, having obtained permission to wash his undergarment, which St. Francis wore very loose, that by wrapping it well around him he might conceal the wound in his pierced side, the said Brother Ruffino examined it diligently and continually found traces of blood on the right side of the garment, by which he knew for certain that the blood came from the wound aforesaid; whereupon St. Francis reproved him for spreading out the garment in order to discover the mark of the wound.

The second way was that the said Brother Ruffino once purposely put his finger into the wound in the side; when St. Francis, for the pain he felt, cried aloud: "God forgive thee, Brother Ruffino, for what thou hast done."

The third way was that this brother once besought St. Francis of his charity to change habits with him, to which the charitable father having consented, although unwillingly, in the exchange of the garments he clearly saw the wound in the right side.

Brother Leo likewise, and many others of the brethren, saw the sacred, holy stigmata during the lifetime of St. Francis; and although for their sanctity these brethren were worthy of all faith upon their simple word, nevertheless, to remove all doubt did they swear upon the Sacred Scriptures that they had seen them plainly.

Certain of the Cardinals also, who enjoyed great familiarity with St. Francis, bore witness to the said sacred, holy stigmata. Even the Sovereign Pontiff, Pope Alexander, when preaching to the people in the presence of the Cardinals, among whom was the holy Brother Bonaventure, himself a Cardinal, affirmed that with his own eyes he had seen the sacred, holy stigmata of St. Francis during his lifetime. And the Lady Jacopa di Settesoli, who was the greatest lady in Rome of her time, and most devout to St. Francis, before and after his death saw and kissed them with great reverence; for she came from Rome to Assisi by divine revelation, at the death of St. Francis; and it came to pass in this way.

A few days before his death, St. Francis lay sick in the bishop's palace at Assisi with certain of his companions, and, notwithstanding his infirmity, he oftentimes sang canticles in honor of Jesus Christ.

One of his companions, therefore, said to him one day: "Father, thou knowest that the citizens of this place have great faith in thee, and account thee to be a holy man. Perhaps therefore they may think that, if thou be what they take thee for, being so grievously sick, thou shouldst think upon death in this thine infirmity, and weep rather than sing. And know that this singing of thine, and of ours whom thou wilt have to sing with thee, is heard by many in the palace and without, forasmuch as this palace is guarded on thine account by many men-at-arms, who may perhaps take scandal thereat. Therefore I think," said this friar, "that thou wilt do well to depart hence, and to return to St. Mary of the Angels; for we are not well here among seculars."

Then St. Francis answered him: "Thou knowest, dearest brother, that two years ago, when we were at Foligno, God revealed the end of my life to thee, and He revealed it to me also—that in this sickness, and in a few days, this my life shall come to an end. And in this revelation God assured me of the remission of all my sins, and of the bliss of paradise. Until I received that revelation, I wept over my sins and at the thought of death; but since I have received it, I have been so full of joy that I can weep no longer; and therefore I sing, and will sing to God, who hath bestowed on me the gift of His grace, and hath certainly promised me the gift of heavenly glory. For our departure hence, it pleaseth me well, and I willingly consent thereto; but find you a way to carry me, for because of my infirmity I cannot walk."

Then the brethren took him up and bore him on their shoulders, and many of the citizens went with them. And coming to a hostel which was on the way, St. Francis said to those who bore him: "Set me down upon the ground, and turn my face towards the city"; and when he was thus turned towards Assisi, he blessed the city with many blessings, saying: "Blessed be thou of God, O holy city, forasmuch as by means of thee many souls shall be saved, and in thee many servants of God shall dwell, and of thy children many shall be elected to eternal life." And when he had said these words, he caused himself to be borne onwards to St. Mary of the Angels; and they carried him to the infirmary, and there laid him down to rest.

Then St. Francis called to him one of his companions, and said to him: "Dearest brother, God has revealed to me that by this sickness, a few days hence, I am to pass from this life; and thou knowest that the devout Lady Jacopa di Settesoli, who is so dear to our Order, would be deeply grieved, should she hear of my death, not to have been present at it; therefore signify to her that, if she desire to see me again in life, she must come hither with all speed."

And the brother made answer: "Too true, Father; for indeed, because of the great devotion she bears thee, most unmeet were it that she should not be present at thy death."

"Go, then," said St. Francis; "bring pen and paper, and write as I shall bid thee." And when he had brought them, St. Francis dictated the letter in the following form: "To the Lady Jacopa, the handmaid of the Lord, Brother Francis, the poor little one of Christ, wishes health and the fellowship of the Holy Ghost in our Lord Jesus Christ. Be it known to thee, most beloved, that Christ our Lord hath by His grace revealed to me the day of my death, which is near at hand. Wherefore, if thou wouldst find me alive, as soon as thou shalt receive this letter, do thou set forth immediately, and come to St. Mary of the Angels; for if thou come not forthwith, thou shalt not find me alive. And bring with thee hair-cloth wherein to wrap my body, and the cerecloth that will be needed for my burial. I pray thee that thou wouldst bring me also some of the food such as thou gavest to me when I was sick at Rome."

Now, while this letter was bring written, it was revealed to St. Francis that the Lady Jacopa was coming to him, and was already near at hand, and that she had brought with her all the things which were asked for in the letter. Having, then, received this revelation, St. Francis bade the brother who was writing to write no more, for it was not needed, but to lay the letter aside; whereupon the brethren greatly marveled why he would not have it finished or sent.

But a short space afterwards, there came a loud knocking at the door, and St. Francis bade the porter open it; which, when he had done, he saw the Lady Jacopa, the most noble of all the ladies of Rome, with two of her sons, who were senators of Rome, and a great company of horsemen, and they entered the house; and the Lady Jacopa went straight to the infirmary to St. Francis. And St. Francis felt great consolation at her coming, and she also rejoiced exceedingly to find him alive, and to speak with him.

Then she declared to him how, being at Rome in prayer, God had revealed to her that his life would shortly come to an end, and that he would send for her and ask those things of her which she had now brought. Then she brought them to St. Francis and gave him to eat; and when he had eaten, and was now much strengthened thereby, the Lady Jacopa knelt at the feet of St. Francis, and with such exceeding devotion kissed and bathed with her tears those feet, marked and adorned with the wounds of Christ, that the brethren who were standing round thought they beheld the Magdalene at the feet of Jesus Christ, and could in no way remove her from him.

At length, after a long space of time they raised her up, and, taking her aside, they asked her how it was she had come thus opportunely, and thus well provided with all things needful for St. Francis, both in his life and for his burial. To this the Lady Jacopa answered, that as she was praying one night in Rome she heard a voice from heaven, which said: "If thou wouldst find St. Francis alive, go without delay to Assisi, and take with thee those things which thou hast been accustomed to prepare for him in sickness, and those which shall be needed for his burial." And, continued the Lady, "As the voice bade me do, so have I done."

So the Lady Jacopa abode at Assisi until St. Francis passed from this life and was buried; and she and all her company paid great honor to his burial, and bore all the cost of it. Then returning to Rome, that noble lady soon afterwards died a holy death, desiring, out of devotion to St. Francis, to be carried to St. Mary of the Angels, and there to be buried; which was done according to her will.

OF THE DAY AND YEAR OF THE DEATH OF SAINT FRANCIS

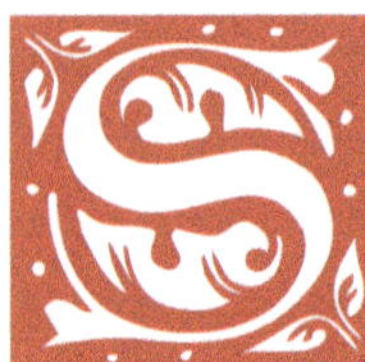

SAINT FRANCIS, the glorious confessor of Christ, passed from this life in the year of our Lord 1226, on Saturday, October 4, and was buried on the Sunday following. He died in the twentieth year of his conversion (that is, from the time when he began to do penance), and the second year after the impression of the sacred, holy stigmata, and the forty-fifth of his age.

St. Francis was canonized in the year 1228 by Pope Gregory IX, who came in person to Assisi for his canonization. And this shall suffice for the fourth consideration.

HOW JEROME, WHO AT FIRST BELIEVED NOT, SAW AND TOUCHED THE SACRED, HOLY STIGMATA OF SAINT FRANCIS

ON THE DEATH of St. Francis, his glorious, sacred stigmata were seen and kissed, not only by the said Lady Jacopa and her company, but by many citizens of Assisi— among others, by a knight of great renown, named Jerome, who had doubted much, and disbelieved them; as St. Thomas disbelieved the wounds of Christ.

And to assure himself and others, he boldly, in the presence both of the brethren and of seculars, moved the nails in the hands and feet, and strongly pressed the wound in the side. By which means he was enabled to bear constant witness to the truth of the miracle, swearing on the Gospels that he had seen and touched the glorious, holy stigmata of St. Francis, the which were seen and touched also by St. Clare and her religious, who were present at his burial.

OF THE FIFTH AND LAST CONSIDERATION OF THE SACRED, HOLY STIGMATA

 HE FIFTH and last consideration is of certain apparitions, revelations, and miracles, which God vouchsafed after the death of St. Francis, in confirmation of the truth of his sacred stigmata, and to certify the day and hour on which Christ gave them to him.

In the year of our Lord, then, 1282, in the month of October, Brother Philip, the minister of Tuscany, by the command of Brother John Buonagrazia, the minister general, required under holy obedience Brother Matthew de Castiglione of Arezzo, a man of great devotion and sanctity, to tell him what he knew of the day and hour in which the sacred, holy stigmata were impressed by Christ on the body of St. Francis, because he had heard that it had been revealed to him.

And Brother Matthew, being constrained by holy obedience, made answer thus: "Being one of the community of Alvernia, last May I was praying in my cell, which is on the spot where the seraph is believed to have appeared. And in my prayer I besought God most devoutly that He would be pleased to make known to some person the day, the hour, and the place in which the sacred, holy stigmata were impressed on the body of St. Francis.

"And persevering thus for a long time in this prayer, St. Francis appeared to me in great glory, and said to me: 'My son, what prayer art thou making to God?' And I said to him: 'Father, I am praying such and such things.' And he said to me: 'I am thy Father Francis. Dost thou know me?' 'Yes, Father,' said I. Then he showed me the sacred, holy stigmata in his hands and feet and side, saying: 'The time is now come when God wills that to be manifested for his glory, which the brethren have not hitherto sought to know. Know, then, that He who appeared to me was no angel, but Jesus Christ Himself under the appearance of a seraph, who, with His own hands, impressed those wounds upon my body, as He Himself received them in His body on the cross; and it was thus.

"'On the day before the Exaltation of the Holy Cross, an angel came to me, and bade me, on the part of God, to prepare to receive with patience whatsoever He should be pleased to send me. And I made answer that I was prepared to receive and endure whatever God should be pleased to appoint for me.

"'And on the following morning, being the morning of Holy Cross day, which in that year fell on a Friday, I left my cell at daybreak in great fervor of spirit, and went to pray in that very spot where thou now dwellest, where I was often accustomed to pray. And as I was praying, there descended through the air with great rapidity the figure of a young man crucified, in the guise of a seraph with six wings. At which marvelous sight I knelt down humbly, and began devoutly to contemplate the unbounded love of Jesus Christ crucified, and the unbounded anguish of His Passion. And such compassion did this spectacle excite within me, that it seemed to me as if I felt that Passion in my own body, and the whole mountain shone like the sun in His presence: and, thus, descending, He came close to me. And standing before me, He spoke to me certain secret words, which I have never yet revealed to any one, but the time is now at hand when they shall be revealed. Then after a little space, Christ departed and returned to heaven, and I found myself thus signed with these wounds. Go, then,' said St. Francis, 'and assure thy minister of these things; for this is the work of God and not of man.'"

"Having said these words, St. Francis blessed me and returned to heaven, accompanied by a great multitude of glorious spirits."

All these things the said Brother Matthew declared that he had seen, not sleeping, but waking. And he made oath that he had thus related them to the said minister in his cell at Florence, when so enjoined by him to do under holy obedience.

IT HAPPENED as a devout and holy friar was reading in the legend of St. Francis the chapter concerning the sacred, holy stigmata, that he began in great anxiety of mind to ponder what those most secret words could be, spoken by the seraph to St. Francis, which he would never reveal to any one in his lifetime.

And he said thus to himself: "St. Francis would never tell these words to any one while he was alive; but now, since his corporal death, he would perhaps reveal them, were he devoutly besought to do so." And from that day forth the fervent friar betook himself to prayer, beseeching God and St. Francis to reveal these words to him; and after persevering for eight years in this prayer, it was at last granted in the following manner.

One day after dinner as he was making his thanksgiving in the church, and remained there praying to this end with greater devotion than usual, and with many tears, he was presently summoned by another friar, by order of the Father Guardian, to go with him to the city on the business of the convent. Not doubting, therefore, that obedience is more meritorious than prayer, he no sooner heard the command of his Superior than he left the church, and went humbly with the brother who called him. And this act of obedience was so pleasing to God, that by it he merited what he had not obtained by all his long years of prayer; for as soon as they had passed through the gate, they met two stranger friars, who seemed as if they had come from a far land, one of whom appeared young, and the other lean and old; and by reason of the bad weather they were both wet and muddy.

On which the obedient friar spoke thus to his companion: "Oh, dearest Brother, if the business on which we are going may brook some little delay, seeing that these stranger brethren have great need of a charitable reception, I pray thee let me first go and wash their feet—and especially those of this ancient brother, and thou mayst wash the feet of the younger—and then we will go upon the business of the convent."

The other friar yielding to the charity of his companion, they returned to the house, and most charitably received those stranger brethren, bringing them into the kitchen to warm and dry themselves at the fire, at which eight other brethren of the place were already warming themselves.

And after they had been awhile at the fire, they took them aside to wash their feet, as they had agreed together to do. Now as the obedient brother was washing the feet of the ancient friar, he beheld on them the marks of the sacred, holy stigmata, and immediately embracing them in joy and wonder, he began to cry: "Either Thou art Christ, or thou art St. Francis!" At that cry, and at these words, the brethren who were at the fire rose up, and drawing near, beheld with great fear and reverence those glorious stigmata. Then the ancient friar suffered them at their earnest desire to behold them clearly, and also to touch and kiss them.

And as they wondered more and more, and scarce believed for joy, he said to them: "Doubt not and fear not, beloved brethren and children; I am your father, Brother Francis, who by the will of God founded three Orders. And inasmuch as this brother, who but now has washed my feet, has been beseeching me these eight years past, and today more fervently than ever, to reveal to him the secret words spoken to me by the seraph when He gave me the stigmata, which words I would never reveal during my lifetime, now by the command of God, for his perseverance and for his prompt obedience by which he left the sweetness of contemplation, I am sent to reveal to him, before you, that which he has asked to know."

Then St. Francis, turning to the friar, said thus: "Know, dearest brother, that when I was on Mount Alvernia, wholly absorbed in the remembrance of the Passion of Christ, in that seraphical apparition I was thus stigmatized by Christ in my body, and then He spoke to me thus: 'Knowest thou what I have done to thee? I have given thee the signs of My Passion that thou mayest be my standard-bearer. And as on the day of My death I descended into limbo, and by virtue of My stigmata drew forth and took with me to paradise all the souls whom I found there, so do I now grant to thee, in order that thou mayest be conformed to Me in death as thou hast been in life, that when thou shalt have passed out of this life, thou shalt descend into purgatory every year on the anniversary of thy death, and by virtue of thy stigmata which I have given thee shalt deliver thence and take with thee to paradise all the souls which thou shalt find there of thy three Orders—Minors, Sisters, and Penitents—with all others whosoever who shall have been devout to thee.' And these words I never told to any one while I was in life."

Having said these words, St. Francis and his companion immediately disappeared. Many brethren heard this related by the eight friars who witnessed the vision and heard the words of St. Francis.

HOW A NOBLE KNIGHT WHO WAS DEVOTED TO SAINT FRANCIS WAS ASSURED OF HIS DEATH AND OF THE SACRED STIGMATA

 NOBLE KNIGHT of Massa di San Pietro, named Landulph, who was most devout to St. Francis, and had received the habit of the Third Order from his hand, was certified thus of his death and of the truth of his sacred, holy and glorious stigmata.

When St. Francis lay on his deathbed, the devil entered into a woman of that place, and cruelly tormented her, and withal made her to speak with such learning and subtlety, that she overcame all the clerks and learned men who came to dispute with her.

Now it came to pass that the devil, departing from her, left her free for the space of two days, after which he returned again, and afflicted her more cruelly than before. Which when Landulph heard he went to the woman, and asked the devil which dwelt within her wherefore he had departed from her for those days, and why he had since returned to torment her worse than before.

And the devil answered thus: "When I left her, I went with all my companions in these parts, being gathered together in great force, to the deathbed of Francis the beggar, to dispute with him, and carry away his soul; but, because it was surrounded and defended by a multitude of angels, far more numerous than we, who carried it straight to heaven, we were forced to retire discomfited; and therefore have I returned to make up to this wretched woman for the peace in which I left her for those days."

Then Landulph conjured him in the name of God to tell him what the truth was regarding the holiness of St. Francis, whom he affirmed to be dead, and for St. Clare, who was still alive.

And the devil answered him: "I must tell thee the truth whether I will or not. The anger of God the Father was so enkindled against the sins of the world that He was ready to pass sentence upon it, and to destroy all men and women from the face of the earth, unless they would repent.

"But Christ His Son, praying for sinners, promised to renew His life and Passion in the person of a man, namely, in St. Francis, a poor mendicant; through whose life and doctrine many throughout the world should be brought back into the way of truth, and many also to penance. And now, to show to the world what He had wrought in St. Francis, He has been pleased that the stigmata of His Passion, which He made to be imprinted on his body during life, should be seen and touched by many since his death.

"In like manner did the Mother of Christ promise to renew her virginal purity and her humility in the person of a woman, to wit, in Sister Clare, that by her example many women might be delivered out of my hands. And the eternal Father, being appeased by these promises, deferred His final sentence."

Then Landulph, wishing to know for certain whether the devil, who is the abode and father of lies, spoke truth in these matters, and especially with regard to the death of St. Francis, sent a faithful servant of his to Assisi, to St. Mary of the Angels, to inquire whether St. Francis were alive or dead.

When the messenger arrived, he found that he was indeed dead, and brought back certain information to his lord that St. Francis had passed from this life on the very day and hour of which the devil had spoken.

ASSING OVER all the miracles of the sacred, holy stigmata of St. Francis, it shall suffice in conclusion of this fifth consideration to relate the following. Pope Gregory IX having some little doubt, as he afterwards related, concerning the wound in the side of St. Francis, the saint one night appeared to him, and raising his right arm a little, discovered to him the wound in his side. He then bade him bring a flask and place it beneath the wound, and when the Pope had done so, he saw it filled to the brim with blood mingled with water, which flowed from the wound; and thereupon all doubt immediately departed from him.

After this, with the concurrence of all the Cardinals, he approved the sacred, holy stigmata of St. Francis by a special bull granted to the friars at Viterbo in the eleventh year of his papacy; and in the following year he issued another, with still more copious privileges.

Pope Nicholas III and Pope Alexander also confirmed the same, with fuller privileges, decreeing that whosoever should deny the sacred, holy stigmata might be proceeded against as a heretic.

And this shall suffice concerning the fifth consideration of the glorious, holy, and sacred stigmata of our father St. Francis, whose life may God give us grace to follow in this world, that by virtue of his glorious stigmata we may deserve to be saved with him in paradise.

TO THE PRAISE OF JESUS CHRIST
AND HIS POOR SERVANT
SAINT FRANCIS!
AMEN.

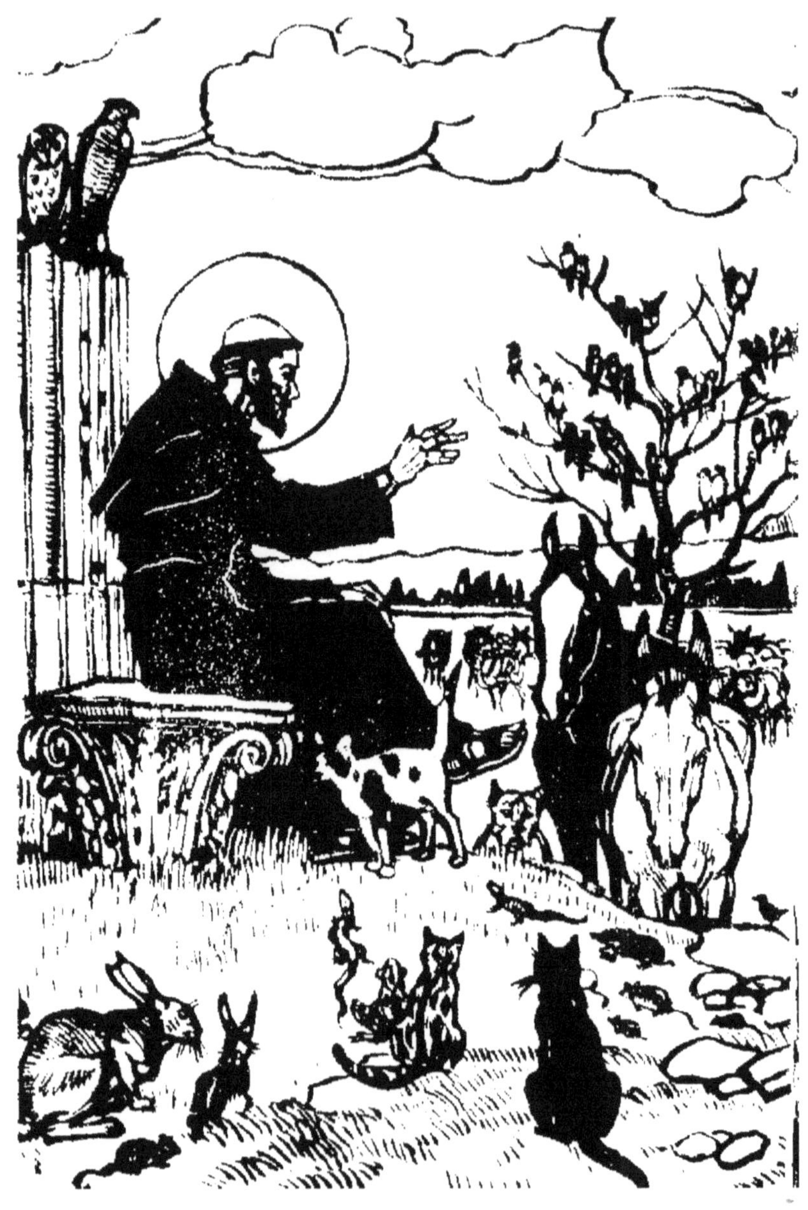